The Health Care Training Handbook

The Jossey-Bass Health Series brings together the most current information and ideas in health care from the leaders in the field. Titles from the Jossey-Bass Health Series include these essential resources:

Customer Service in Health Care: A Grassroots Approach to Creating a Culture of Excellence *Kristin M. Baird* Here is a practical, step-by-step plan for strengthening the customer service initiative within an organization. This title outlines a practical plan, including the needed incentives, for successfully creating cultural transformation. An AHA Press/Jossey-Bass publication.

Breakthrough Performance: Accelerating the Transformation of Health Care Organizations *Ellen J. Gaucher, Richard J. Coffey* Two acclaimed quality management gurus show health care practitioners a step-by-step guide on inspiring the shared sense of urgency that is key to effective and successful innovation and creating the organizational alignment that is crucial to achieving breakthrough performance.

Honoring Patient Preferences: A Guide to Complying with Multicultural Patient Requirements *Anne Knights Rundle, Maria Carvalho, Mary Robinson, editors* Here is an indispensable manual for professionals caring for patients from diverse religious and cultural backgrounds. Sponsored by Children's Hospital in Boston—the hospital voted number one in pediatrics nine years in a row by *U.S. News and World Report*—this essential guide contains detailed, practical information for working with dozens of religious and cultural groups, as well as a systematic approach to meeting Joint Commission on Accreditation standards and a key-word searchable CD-ROM containing the entire text of the book.

Managing Diversity in Health Care: Cultural Diversity as a Strategic Advantage *Lee Gardenswartz, Anita Rowe* This essential handbook provides the necessary knowledge and tools to become more responsive to culturally diverse patient and staff populations. The authors show how to build diverse teams, deal with the thorny issues of prejudice and bias, and communicate effectively within a diverse health care setting.

Managing Diversity in Health Care Manual: Proven Tools and Activities for Leaders and Trainers *Lee Gardenswartz, Anita Rowe* Now it's easy to do diversity training—along with team development, customer service, conflict resolution, and community relations. This versatile collection of activities, resources, and training materials is designed to facilitate a successful training program in any kind of health care organization. Reinforces the concepts presented in *Managing Diversity in Health Care.* Includes a disk for creating customized training agendas.

Total Customer Satisfaction: A Comprehensive Approach for Health Care Providers *Stephanie G. Sherman, V. Clayton Sherman* This systematic guide reports the breakthrough methods used by award-winning hospitals and health care organizations to achieve top-rated national status in customer satisfaction.

Collaborating to Improve Community Health: Workbook and Guide to Best Practices in Creating Healthier Communities and Populations *Kathryn Johnson, Wynne Grossman, Anne Cassiby, editors* Here is the essential resource that shows how key players from local governments, businesses, health care organizations, school boards, churches, and police departments can be turned into a team, working together to improve their communities. The editors have compiled the accumulated wisdom of top consultants and practitioners into a wealth of resources—including worksheets, guidelines, overhead slides, and case studies—designed to help every community implement a workable plan of action.

The Health Care Training Handbook

Kathryn Wall

JOSSEY-BASS
A Wiley Company
San Francisco

This publication is designed to provide accurate and authoritative information in regard to the subject matter covered. It is sold with the understanding that the publisher is not engaged in rendering professional services. If professional advice or other expert assistance is required, the services of a competent professional person should be sought.

Jossey-Bass books and products are available through most bookstores. To contact Jossey-Bass directly, call (888) 378-2537, fax to (800) 605-2665, or visit our website at www.josseybass.com.

Substantial discounts on bulk quantities of Jossey-Bass books are available to corporations, professional associations, and other organizations. For details and discount information, contact the special sales department at Jossey-Bass.

 Manufactured in the United States of America on recycled paper.

Library of Congress Cataloging-in-Publication Data

Wall, Kathryn.
    The health care training handbook / Kathryn Wall.—1st ed.
        p. cm. — (Jossey-Bass health series)
    Includes index.
    ISBN 0-7879-4565-X (hardcover : alk. paper)
    1. Medical personnel—Training of—Handbooks, manuals, etc.   I. Title.   II. Series.
RA440.W35 2000
610'.71'1—dc21   00-023206

FIRST EDITION
HC Printing   10 9 8 7 6 5 4 3 2 1

CONTENTS

PREFACE
THE NEED

Over the course of the last decade, the need for professional training practitioners in health care has dramatically increased. Myriad regulatory requirements, such as those of the Joint Commission on Accreditation of Healthcare Organizations (JCAHO) and the federal Occupational Safety and Health Administration (OSHA), the complexity of technology (PET scans and new procedures for caring for patients), and the often-limited experience of employees has forced health care organizations to invest in training and organizational development as a means of addressing these issues in the changing world of health care.

The price to be paid for not addressing these issues can be exorbitant. Recently, for example, most health care organizations have been mandated by the federal government to provide all employees with training in the area of compliance. The cost for not providing this training would in part be a cutback in the funding for Medicare and Medicaid patients. Tough penalties for lack of training!

Additionally, to compete with other health care organizations, hospitals and medical centers have begun to recognize the benefits of creating a competent workforce. The task of creating this workforce has been placed in the hands of training practitioners. Health care organizations such as the University of Chicago Hospital, Holy Cross, and Partners Health have seen the bottom-line impact of investing in training. For example, one Midwestern hospital invested in customer-service training for staff and raised their customer satisfaction results more than 90 percent. Training can yield powerful results! The question, then, is who will deliver the training, and what will the quality be?

Traditionally health care organizations have enlisted clinical experts for the role of training practitioners. For example, a floor nurse might be assigned to train new staff on how to give a patient an injection. Yet this nurse might lack formal education in training and instructional design. In fact, it is not uncommon for clinical educators to design clinical programs without ever using such basic training design skills as a training needs assessment, learning plans, and evaluations. The consequence can be less-than-effective training for staff. In these changing times, clinical experts are also being asked to branch out into other skill development areas, such as leadership development, supervisory skills, quality, and customer service.

With the above facts in mind, I see today the need for a formalized approach to training these clinical practitioners in the basics of the training and development profession. By learning the skills of training design, delivery, and evaluation, they are able to assess needs, determine appropriate approaches, and deliver effective clinical and management development training to health care staff.

THE AUDIENCE

The Health Care Training Handbook is designed to help health care trainers optimize resources and achieve quality results in all aspects of training, from clinical education to leadership and management development and to employee training. It is designed for the health care trainer who comes from a clinical discipline and lacks the skills of training and organizational development. It is also designed for the training professional who is new to health care. This is the professional who knows traditional training yet is unfamiliar with the medical setting and client base, and who may be asked to design a clinical skills program but has no clinical experience.

This book addresses the needs of both audiences by exploring the basics of training assignments, design, and delivery, as well as offering clinical and non-clinical examples. The reader receives answers to specific questions as well as tools and examples that have been designed for health care applications.

THE TOPIC

The Health Care Training Handbook covers topics ranging from exploration of health care and training trends to the basic steps of designing and implementing a training program. Chapter One explores the key trends facing health care and training; it encompasses the unique demands I have faced as a health care trainer. Chapter Two takes a look at how health care organizations are typically organizing their training departments to respond to trends and the needs of their clients—in particular, the impact of the JCAHO on the structure and focus of training.

Chapters Three through Six provide a practical how-to approach to training basics: conducting a needs assessment in Chapter Three, designing a training program in Chapter Four, training delivery in Chapter Five, and evaluating training in Chapter Six. Each chapter is chock full of tools and examples that I have used in both clinical and nonclinical training.

The final chapters focus on key issues of training and the training professional. Chapter Seven reviews the obstacles to training and ways to overcome them. Chapter Eight covers how to position training and yourself for success. The book wraps up in Chapter Nine with a resource section giving references that I have found to be of great assistance.

THE SEQUENCE

You may read this book in chapter sequence, or you may go to the chapter that addresses your specific needs. However, if you are new to training and development, I recommend that you read the chapters on the basics of training (Three, Four, Five, and Six) in order. The process of designing and implementing training is sequential, and you will reap the most benefit if you read the content in this order.

Finally, I wish you good luck in your training endeavors. This is an exciting time to be part of a dynamic industry and a distinguished profession.

ACKNOWLEDGMENTS

It took a team approach to make *The Health Care Training Handbook* a reality. First, to my team at Virtua Health—Beth Boland Rollins, Debbie Malone,

Jennifer Szybiak, Jane-Alyse Von Ohlen, Cheryl Onorato, and Kim Packer—for their ideas and suggestions on the book's content and format. Special thanks to Roxanne Galanti for patiently proofreading, editing, and typing, often with short deadlines; Roxanne, you were a positive force behind this effort. Thanks also to Ed Dunn for his encouragement, helpful ideas, insights, and humor.

At Jossey-Bass, I want to thank the team of Andrew Pasternack, Danielle Neary, and Katie Crouch for helping me, as a first-time author, understand the world of publishing, and for extending resources that made this book a reality.

Maryanne Koschier, my developmental editor, provided me with incredible support blended with specific suggestions and encouragement. Thank you for helping me find my voice—your help is the true reason this book is a reality.

Lastly, I want to thank my family for their unfailing support: my sisters, Ann Wall and Susan Datta; my brother-in-law, Matt Datta; and nephews Sam Datta, Will Datta, and Ben Winstead. This book is dedicated to the two people who have always been there for me, my parents, Floyd and Jean Wall. You taught me to believe all things are possible.

THE AUTHOR

Kathryn Wall is the assistant vice president of organizational effectiveness for Virtua Health. Prior to joining Virtua Health, she served as director of training and organizational development for West Virginia University Hospitals, and as a senior trainer for Washington Hospital Center. She has been a training consultant to a variety of other health care organizations and recently coauthored two articles on organizational transformation. She has presented at several national conferences on topics related to health care training. Her interest and current areas of focus include organizational transformation, change management, development of learning teams, and alignment of organizational culture for performance and results.

Wall earned her B.A. degree (1980) in art history from the University of Virginia and her M.A. (1985) in human resources development from George Washington University. She also completed the Fellows program in change management (1995) at Johns Hopkins University.

She is a member of the American Society for Training and Development and has served as a health care forum leader nationally as the organizational development special interest group director for the Philadelphia local chapter. She is also a member of the Human Resources Planning Society and the Organization Development Network.

The Health Care Training Handbook

Major Trends in Health Care and the World of the Worker

It is hard to imagine any industry in the past ten years that has been more volatile than health care. Surely no health care worker has failed to notice how fast and furious the changes are—everything from shortened hospital stays, sicker and more complicated patients, and declining reimbursement rates to new and complex technology and impending mergers and acquisitions. In this chapter, we discuss the trends within the health care arena, such as ongoing reform, mergers and acquisitions, new care delivery models, technology, preventive models, decreased reimbursement and regulatory requirements, and the major trends in the world of the worker in general and how they affect trainers in the health care training field.

CURRENT DEVELOPMENTS IN HEALTH CARE

Health care trainers need to realize the developments in the industry affect what training is needed and how it is delivered. Here are some of the most important trends in health care.

Ongoing Reform of the Health Care System

Congress is attempting to confront problems of Medicaid reform, Medicare, and the uninsured. In addition, legislators have been forced to create new policies and laws, such as defining access to specialty care or enacting a patient's bill of rights, to determine the type of care patients should receive as a means of answering the many critics of managed care. Recently, the evening news programs discussed new legislation that would affect whether patients should call their HMO or managed care company prior to dialing 911. Imagine a patient in a crisis having to have her insurance company mandate when and if she should seek emergency care! Critics have charged managed care companies with denying care for patients by limiting the types and kinds of reimbursement or the amount of payment for services and care that hospitals and physicians can receive. Some hospitals have added new positions such as governmental liaisons to lobby legislators on their behalf. Over the past year alone, I have attended at least five legislative update sessions at which hospital associations presented an overview of pending legislation and the effects on health care. With health care accounting for more than 17 percent of the gross national product, legislators and health care leaders will continue to focus on resolving the complexity of health care issues.

Mergers and Acquisitions

Hospitals continue to consolidate. With each passing year, fewer independent hospitals remain. In their place are ever-larger networks of hospitals and health service organizations, such as physician practices designed to address the continuum of care encompassing home-based health; long-term, subacute, or transitional caring; hospitals; longer-term care facilities. Specialized rehabilitation (such as spinal cord, head injuries, or stroke) has arisen. Networks and affiliations are designed to link the services of two health care organizations to give the patient lifetime solutions to health care needs. A recent statistic says that over the course of the next five years, 75 percent of all hospitals will enter into an affiliation. This certainly illustrates the scope of change in store for health care workers today.

New Care Delivery Models

In the last few years, most health care systems have redefined their delivery models or the process they use to organize and deliver care. In many hospitals, patients are grouped to units by like diagnosis; for example, oncology surgery patients are now housed together. In this unit, the delivery model might include an on-site pharmacy and radiology department and nurses who have significant oncology experience.

As health care organizations refocus on patients and their needs, hospitals redesign systems, processes, and roles. For instance, support functions (housekeeping, transport, dietary functions) are grouped together for a multiskilled worker or support associate's role. In one mid-Atlantic hospital, the admissions process was redesigned to focus on the convenience of the patient. Instead of patients' waiting in an admissions department, they are now directed to their rooms, where an admission clerk comes to them to gather patient and insurance information.

Another impact of redesign is in staffing mixes and ratios. This refers to the number of nursing, ancillary, and support personal necessary to care for each patient. In critical-care units, nurses are typically assigned fewer patients because they are sicker and require in-depth nursing care. In many respects, redesign efforts are also intended to help hospitals design the best system for delivering cost-effective care. These efforts may require higher ratios and different mixes. It is not unheard of for nurses to have seven, eight, or nine patients assigned on a medical floor. This has led to employee concern about jobs and roles in the wake of these redesign efforts.

Technology

Technology has had an impact on many aspects of health care, and in the next few years it will continue to revolutionize medicine. Advances in computer-assisted radiological equipment enable physicians to receive 3-D pictures of organs within the body. Information systems create paperless medical records. Soon everyone may be able to carry his medical history to the physician and hospital on a record the size of a credit card. Technology is indubitably changing how hospitals deliver care.

In my own health care system, we are using the Internet to monitor diabetes patients. We work daily to ensure that these patients perform tests each day. This program also enables them to receive current information about their disease.

Whether through monitoring patients via the Internet or linking medical records electronically, health care invests in and expects more from the information technology department.

Wellness and Preventive Models

An increasing number of health care organizations are refocusing their resources in the areas of preventive medicine and wellness. Examples include yearly reminders for mammograms and prostate screens, disease-specific education programs, and exercise and weight-reduction programs. These new programs and services extend beyond the walls of a hospital and into the patients' homes.

In many respects, preventing disease is a new focus for today's health care organization. Traditionally, health care concentrated on sickness; hospitals and physicians were paid to take care of ill patients. It did not matter how long a patient was hospitalized or the level of care required; they were paid. As the cost of health care rises, insurance companies limit payments to hospitals and physicians. Now it makes sense to keep patients healthy to reduce the cost of caring for them. Therefore, hospitals and physicians continue to invest in wellness as a preventive measure for their patients.

Decreasing Reimbursement

A decline in charity care and reduced reimbursement rates from insurance or health maintenance organizations (HMOs) has led to emphasis on reducing costs, and in some cases services. In 1998, more than seventy million Americans were enrolled in HMOs. This enrollment has grown by leaps and bounds, with more than twelve million Americans signing on since 1994. In many respects, HMOs determine the type of health care received, including the length of stay and the type and scope of procedures and tests. Because they have relinquished control of these important decisions, hospitals have lost money. In my own hospital, we lost more than $300,000 within three months in denied days (days that insurance companies refuse to pay for). In response to such developments, hospitals are reducing staff, services, and programs.

Regulatory Requirements

As HMOs and managed care companies control the purse strings, regulatory requirements continue to mandate the level of care. Accrediting organizations, such as the Joint Commission on Accreditation of Hospitals, are requiring hospitals to meet high quality standards. The accreditation process encompasses everything from review of employee records (to ensure employees have received proper orientation) to review of the physician credentialing process. This accreditation is crucial for hospitals; without it, many managed care companies do not allow their subscribers to use the hospital or its services. The federal government is also mandating that all organizations have a compliance program; it requires training on the organization's code of ethics. This regulation is a requirement for ongoing Medicare and Medicaid funding.

Quality also has an important role in being continuously ready to meet regulatory requirements. In the last ten years, health care has embraced the total-quality-management philosophy as a means of illustrating the organization's commitment to delivering high-quality care. For example, most patient incidents such as falls are investigated using quality tools.

For training and organizational practitioners, these trends paint a challenging picture of the future of health care. Still, it is an exciting time to be in health care. Whether helping organizations adapt to change, teaching caregivers how to provide care for various illnesses, or training new residents, health care offers a trainer incredible rewards. Every time I walk through a hospital, I am reminded of the true reward of my work: helping caregivers give the best care in the best way to make a difference in the life of a patient. No other industry can affect people so profoundly.

TRENDS IN THE WORLD OF THE WORKER

Let us now look at the major changes affecting the workplace, and then review the implications for you as a professional in the health care training field. As I see them, the major changes are:

- The worker's need for technology skills
- Workforce diversity

- Continuous process improvement and performance improvement
- Restructuring or reorganization
- Changing trainer skills and training services
- The rise of learning organizations

Worker's Need for Technology Skills

With almost half of the new jobs created in the last ten years requiring education beyond high school (more than 40 percent of workers now use computers as part of their jobs), tomorrow's workforce needs to adapt to handling new technologies. On the day I wrote this, for example, my organization created a computer operations competency stating the minimum level of performance workers need in our organization. This basic competency requires employees to turn on and operate their computer, access and use department-specific software, retrieve e-mail, and perform basic word processing functions.

Workforce Diversity

Today's workforce is significantly more diverse than before. In particular, there is a significant increase in minorities, women, and older workers filling the jobs of today (and tomorrow). If we look closely at this issue, we see that trends point to growth in the presence of Hispanics and Asians in the labor force. This stems from increased immigration. One interesting fact is that each year more than 820,000 people come to the United States, and better than two-thirds are of working age. Additionally, not only is the number of women who work outside the home continuing to increase but the workforce is definitely aging. The average age of today's worker is forty-five.

In health care, the effect of the aging workforce is particularly evident with registered nurses. Today's staff nurses may not have the education desired to continue meeting the needs of the patient.

Continuous Process Improvement and Performance Improvement

There is great emphasis today on improving the performance of employees and systems to increase organizational effectiveness and efficiency. Colleagues across the country are pointing to performance improvement as a critical success factor. Even JCAHO is focusing on performance improvement as a key driver of the accreditation process.

Restructuring or Reorganization

As organizations try to increase their efficiency and effectiveness, restructuring and reorganization continue to play a key role in today's business environment. With more than twenty-five hundred hospitals currently in merged or integrated systems and more organizations merging daily, workers not only confront learning new systems and organizations but also face the risk of being let go. Most organizations today outsource at least one business service or activity.

The Rise of Learning Organizations

Learning continues to be a key component of success for the coming century. Most organizations consider creation of a learning organization a crucial driver of success. The ability to learn and share best practices is a core need for today's (and future) leaders. For organizations in the next century, capitalizing on intellectual capital means the organization uses the collective knowledge of its workers to increase the performance of individuals and the organization. This sharing includes databases or systems where solutions are shared, identifying employee experts within the organization to serve as consultants to other parts of the organization, and using interactive software with which several people can work on issues at the same time.

IMPLICATIONS FOR HEALTH CARE

Just looking at how the world of the worker has changed in the last ten years tells us that likewise the roles, skills, and delivery modes of training must change also. Today's health care trainer performs a multitude of duties. Let me illustrate by sharing how my own role has changed over the last few years.

First of all, I have moved from a training specialist role to that of chief learning officer. Instead of reacting to individual requests for training, my time is spent in spotting the performance issues within my hospital system and proactively devising learning solutions. In determining how to provide mandatory training in the areas of infection control and safety, I have explored such alternative delivery methods as computer-based training as a way of reaching employees at the worksite cost-effectively. I am also working on setting up a learning strategy that supports the organization's vision, mission, and values through innovative learning solutions: initiating learning teams to bring managers together to dialogue and learn about best practices, such as how to implement quality standards in our health care organizations.

Secondly, I now spend a great deal of time as an internal consultant. On a recent day, I consulted with a manager about increasing team performance, worked with a team on resolving conflict, and gave a senior leader feedback on his style. Whether it is understanding the need for technology, serving as a performance consultant, or setting a learning strategy, my focus is shaped by the impact of these trends in health care.

Let's take a look at specific implications of these trends for you, the training professional.

The Need for Technology Skills

As we discussed earlier, technology is revolutionizing all aspects of health care. Employees are using computers for clinical record keeping, as well as diagnosing illness with sophisticated equipment and the Internet. Recently, for example, a family member was diagnosed with a rare disease. The Internet was our family's first source of information on treatment options. This allowed us to ask the physician specific questions about the illness, treatment, and prognosis.

All health care employees—nurses, pharmacists, respiratory therapists, dietitians, and so on—need to be computer literate and proficient in technological skills. This need increases the amount and kind of computer training that health care offers. It is not uncommon on any given day, in any hospital, to see classes on everything from clinical recording-keeping systems to physician ordering systems or drug-dispensing systems. In my own organization, we use computer-based training to provide clinical and regulatory training.

Workforce Diversity

Workforce diversity extends beyond race and ethnicity to gender and age. Health care trainers can show organizations how to capitalize on these differences. I was recently asked to present training on building a culture of respect. The focus of the program was how to understand and respect people who are ethnically and culturally diverse. Designed for managers, the topics included creating a code of respect and how to address disrespectful behavior among employees. Additionally, the rise of immigration might also point to the need for English-speaking classes or basic skills training.

Continuous Process Improvement and Performance Improvement

At the beginning of my training career, I used training as the solution to any and every problem. "Patients have been complaining about employee so-and-so," someone would tell me; "do you have a training program that might help?" My response was typically an impassioned yes. In the past few years, though, as organizations have focused more on continuous process improvement, my role has also moved toward performance consultant. Moving into this role has forced me to identify and diagnose performance problems and use a variety of approaches—which may or may not include training. Today, when requests come in, I first examine the need for training. By asking managers to describe the performance problem and using questions to analyze the expected and current behavior, I can determine if training is the best solution.

Restructuring or Reorganization

Restructuring has led to more mergers and affiliations. Health care workers are increasingly concerned about job security and are suffering from low employee morale. Health care trainers must quantify the benefits of training; does it deliver what it is supposed to? Mergers and affiliations create the need to mold two differing organizational cultures into one. Health care trainers can spearhead this effort as well. They should be aware of morale and how it affects the type of training that is delivered.

As my own system merges with another, a central theme is how to use the role of training to help support the vision, mission, and values. One way training supports this initiative is through developing a training program that focuses on leading with vision, mission, and values, taught by our senior executives.

Changing Trainer Skills and Training Services

The size and scope of training services are changing. Although some corporations are downsizing or outsourcing services, health care shows renewed interest in training and organizational development services as a key driver of employee satisfaction and more. Many leaders are beginning to recognize the power of strong managers and employees and are reinvesting in their development.

Hospitals are refocusing training services to include a performance-consultant model, in which trainers are asked to help business units improve performance and ultimately influence the bottom line. Trainers in my organization serve as partners with managers and employees in designing solutions that may not require training; as an example, a clinical education coordinator worked with the laboratory to develop a process to decrease errors in labeling tubes. This new framework is requiring trainers to learn new skills. In addition to classic design and delivery skills, today's trainers also have to understand the organization's business goals, diagnose problems, and develop usable solutions.

Learning Organizations

Health care trainers should act as advocates and experts on learning and learning organizations. The process of sharing information and best practices and determining new ways to learn guides health care organizations in achieving their goals. One innovative technique I use is to create leadership learning teams. These cross-functional learning teams determine their own learning goals and select methods that support individual and team learning. Whether it is discussing a case or reading a book, it is a powerful process.

CONCLUSION

In this chapter, we have explored such trends in health care as ongoing reform, mergers and acquisitions, new care delivery models, burgeoning technology, and decreased reimbursement. We looked at how these trends are affecting health care, and particularly training. Then we reviewed the trends in training (technology, workforce diversity, performance improvement, and changing structure and roles for training). We examined how these trends have an impact on today's health care trainer. The reality is that the once separate worlds of training and health care continue to merge, integrate, and influence one another. Health care trainers of the future will not only need to develop some of the same skills as the health care workers they serve but also have to merge these skills into training and organizational development practices.

In the next chapter, we look at the organizational structure of the health care training department and the role of the trainer.

Organizational Structure of Health Care Training Departments and the Role of Trainers

N ow that we've looked at the dynamic changes that are affecting health care and the training professional, let's see how health care organizations are typically setting up their training departments to respond to these overall trends and to the needs of their clients, that is, the administrative, operational, and medical staff of their health care facility. In particular, we will see how JCAHO accreditation requirements influence health care programs and approaches. This discussion is of particular interest to you if you are new to health care training. If you are a health care professional, you may well find the evolution of training department structures useful as you become part of a centralized learning and training division.

Next, the chapter focuses on discussion of the roles, responsibilities, and learning news of the training professional in health care. The emphasis is on the similarities and differences in roles for the two kinds of trainer this handbook addresses: the clinical educator and the employee or management development training specialist.

Finally, the chapter closes with an examination of the learning needs of both kinds of health care trainer.

CURRENT ORGANIZATIONAL STRUCTURE: A PERSONAL LOOK

To begin my review of health care training structures in today's environment, I turn to my own current organization. I am the assistant vice president of organizational effectiveness for a large community health care system. I report to the vice president of human resources and support the entire organization. With more than seven thousand employees spread over hospitals, long-term care facilities, ambulatory surgery centers, physician offices, home health agencies, and administrative and corporate sites, the role of my department is to serve the varied education and training needs of all employees in the system. To accomplish this, the organizational effectiveness function comprises four units: corporate clinical education, employee and management development, organizational development, and the administrative unit.

The corporate clinical education unit is made up of a coordinator of clinical education and two clinical educators. These educators are clinical experts, nurses who have translated their nursing practice into a training department. They are responsible for systemwide clinical education for nurses, ancillary, and support personnel. Systemwide education is defined as those educational programs that are needed throughout the system, such as clinical orientation.

Another example of their work is documentation training. In this case, the documentation or patient charting process was changed. This affected all clinical employees, and we in organizational effectiveness worked to plan the education for more than two thousand employees. Although the organizational effectiveness staff is small in number, they are supported by divisional clinical education representatives that coordinate site-specific education, as well as adjunct faculty, for example, experts in critical care involved in the critical-care course.

It is worth noting that in our current model, the divisional education representatives report directly to their respective organizational units. This has led to some confusion over corporate versus divisional education. To address this matter, we are reexamining this role and determining how to better support divisional units.

The second unit is employee and management development, encompassing the entire organization and all clients, physician offices, patient accounting, and patient-care units. In my organization, along with one training specialist (an expert in training and development) I support this function. The employee and management development unit is responsible for designing and delivering nonclinical training for employees and managers. This includes new-employee orientation, customer service, and management programs such as coaching and counseling, performance management, and recognition strategies. Because we have limited staff, we also support this area by using consultants who serve as adjunct faculty.

The third unit is organizational development. This is where I spend most of my time. Organizational development is designed to increase the effectiveness of individual, units, teams, and the organization. It focuses on all client groups within the organization, from senior management to front-line managers, nursing, and home health. Typical projects include team building, conflict resolution, strategic planning, and facilitation. I also support this area with organizational development consultants whom I engage for a particular project.

The last area is our administrative unit. Attending to administrative work, this unit is responsible for program marketing, registration, and record keeping, as well as material preparation. Examples of the staff's work are designing program marketing materials such as flyers and brochures, designing participant workbooks, and recording and documenting attendance.

As you can see from my example, my department serves the entire organization. The clinical education arm is focused on clinical services, but they have also extended support, when needed, to any project or area. Now that we see how my organization works, let's look at the commonalities that exist among health care training department structures.

SOME BASICS OF TRAINING DEPARTMENT STRUCTURES

In looking at health care training in organizational structures across the country, it is easy to see commonalities. First, there are two basic structures: the parallel structure, where clinical or nursing education are units separate from employee and management development; and the integrated department that combines clinical, management, and employee development.

The parallel structure is a traditional health care model. In this type of structure, clinical and nonclinical units run in parallel. With this model, clinical education reports to nursing or clinical services and normally undertakes clinical and regulatory training. There is some variation; in certain cases, centralized clinical training houses educators in one unit, and they may have client groups that correspond to their specialty. For example, a colleague at a university teaching hospital reported that clinical educators were assigned client groups, such as critical care, medical-surgical, or perioperative. These educators worked together to plan programs jointly, but they also spent a lot of their time doing customized training for their client groups.

Another variation was reported from a community health care organization. In this case, the clinical education unit was decentralized and educators were assigned to specific units. They worked specifically with their units to design customized training.

Running parallel to the clinical unit is a training-and-development department. In this model, the department is responsible for nonclinical education. These trainers provide "soft skills" training, as well as orientation. Organizational development may or may not report within the unit as part of the department. Some hospitals have created new units that focus on organizational transformation and organizational development. I recently saw a position in the local paper for a "director of culture change," with this position leading the organizational development unit. Reporting structures in these units vary, but normally the unit reports to human resources. I have seen cases where it reports to the CEO, COO, or CFO. Another variation on this model is to add other training, such as community education, patient education, continued medical education, and information-system training.

Second is the integrated training model. Here, all aspects of training are organized under the leadership of one training-and-development professional. In a large health care system in Florida, the training unit encompassed all clinical education, management development, information development, community and patient education, continued medical education, organizational development, and library services. The director of this area reported directly to the CEO.

The integrated model is the direction that many health care organizations are taking. One of the key benefits is cost-effectiveness, reducing duplication of effort. Also, and more important, it allows all education services to be connected, permitting flexibility in assigning resources to the greatest needs.

CHANGES OVER THE YEARS: A PERSPECTIVE

Health care training organizational structures are different from those of ten years ago. A colleague of mine who worked in a major metropolitan hospital described her training organization in the early 1990s. The training department's major component had long been a clinical one: training respiratory therapists, nurses, and physical therapists. Management and professional development training was a relatively new area when she joined the so-called soft side of training and development. There was one training director for both groups, but for all intents and purposes they functioned as separate and distinct units. Then, thanks to JCAHO requirements, a new division was formed: total quality management (TQM). The goal was to improve the operational processes of the medical hospital, and to improve patient satisfaction with health care delivery.

The TQM program was to focus on every department and involved all levels of staff, including the CEO and the senior management board. Soon thereafter, the TQM division became the driving force for all training-and-development activities at the hospital, and former training departments began reporting directly to this division.

I tell this story because it illustrates the evolution of health care training structures over the last several years—an evolution that continues today. It also illustrates the impact that JCAHO requirements have on health care training, one that it is important to know about as we go deeper into our discussion of health care training. Let me now review some basics of what we know about JCAHO.

JCAHO AND ITS IMPACT ON TRAINING

The Joint Commission on Accreditation of Healthcare Organizations (JCAHO) focuses primarily on improving the quality of care provided to patients. Its charge is accreditation of health care organizations and improvement in organizational performance. It has developed rigorous standards and performance measures which are evaluated in a triennial survey process.

JCAHO has an enormous task: evaluation of more than eighteen thousand health care organizations. For these organizations in turn, it is an immense task to continuously address the performance requirements of the standards. An example of a standard is to promote healthy behaviors and support patient-family involvement. The hospital would then have to show how it supports this standard.

JCAHO has a long and impressive history. Founded in 1910, with the charge of creating hospital standardization, over the next several years the mission was expanded with introduction of minimum standards for hospitals and the survey process, which began in 1918.

JCAHO gradually expanded its scope and services. In the 1960s, long-term-care accreditation began. In the 1970s, ambulatory health care standards were established, and the survey cycle was changed from two to three years. In the 1980s, hospice was added, and JCAHO introduced a tailored survey approach. In addition, the indicator measurement system, a performance monitor, was started. In the 1990s, JCAHO reorganized around important patient-care and organizational functions and shifted the focus to measures that reflect the organization's actual performance. The ORYN system (the Joint Commission's initiative to integrate performance measures into the accreditation process) was also introduced to use outcomes and other performance measures in the accreditation process. Beginning this year, JCAHO began to offer accreditation services to international health care organizations.

Several of the JCAHO standards have a strong educational and training focus. For instance, JCAHO requires employees to have training in these areas:

- Fire safety
- Bloodborne pathogens
- Age-appropriate care
- Recognizing signs of abuse
- Patient confidentiality
- Conscious sedation
- Advance directives

To address these requirements, trainers create training in these areas. Titles might include Patient Rights and Advanced Directives; Elder Abuse; Conscious Sedation; Fire, Safety, and Emergency Preparedness; and Caring for the Neonate. Therefore, it is imperative that a health care worker have access to and be familiar with JCAHO requirements. Also, before designing a course, the trainer must consult the guidelines.

In terms of the organizational training structure, JCAHO may have a direct or indirect effect on the organizational training structure. In the previous example about my colleague and changing perspectives, we saw a health care organization that used JCAHO as a key driver in designing the training organization. In the organizations that I have been a part of, JCAHO played an indirect role in the training focus. Because of JCAHO's major role, my organization has created a quality unit where the JCAHO staff is housed. Preparing the accreditation process requires significant work for the entire organization, and every department has a role in ensuring a successful accreditation process. In most cases, a quality leader assumes responsibility for the preparation process, and trainers serve as consultants to the JCAHO leader and the quality team.

ROLES AND RESPONSIBILITIES OF HEALTH CARE TRAINERS

Now that we have reviewed current trends in health care training department structures and JCAHO, we turn our attention to the roles and responsibilities of the two kinds of health care trainer: the clinical educator and the employee and management development training specialist.

Clinical educators, as we have previously discussed, are usually experts in a clinical specialty, such as nursing, physical therapy, radiology. They are normally selected for an educator role because of their excellent technical skills.

Roxanne, a Clinical Educator

Roxanne is an RN who has five years of experience on the medical-surgical unit. Over the years, she has served as preceptor or mentor to many of the new nurses on the unit. Recently, she was selected as the unit's new clinical educator. In her new role, she is responsible for orienting new employees to the unit and offering education or in-services on a variety of disease-specific topics. For example, she recently held sessions on care of diabetic patients, wound care, and new drug updates.

Roxanne also works one-to-one with staff, supporting their learning and educational goals. You might find her in a patient's role with a new nurse while showing her how to insert an IV, or working with a nursing aide on giving a patient a bath.

In addition to unit-specific training, Roxanne is also responsible for ensuring that the staff meets annual competency requirements. For her unit, she prepares training for competencies related to understanding the symptoms of abuse or the hospital's restraint standards.

The second type of health care educator is the employee and management development trainer specialist. For this trainer, health care might be a new industry. The training specialist usually has an academic background in the field of adult learning or training and development. Her academic preparation includes courses on assessing needs, designing training programs, delivery skills, and evaluation. As a health care trainer, she normally conducts training for clinical and nonclinical employees in areas such as customer service, business skills, and management and leadership skills.

Sam, an Employee and Management Development Training Specialist

Sam, a recent graduate of the George Washington University training-and-development program, is an employee and management development training specialist with a community health care system. Sam does training in a variety of employee and management development skills area. Last month, he designed programs for employees on adapting to workplace training, teamwork, time management, and for managers in the areas of performance-appraisal skills and coaching and counseling.

In addition to organizational training programs, Sam also provides customized training solutions for specific departments. He recently offered stress management for the linen services department and is currently planning a program on communication styles for the critical care unit. Besides training, Sam does one-on-one counseling for managers and employees in preparing development plans or improving skills.

IMPLICATION OF LEARNING NEEDS OF TRAINERS

The stories of Roxanne and Sam serve to illustrate not only the new roles of the trainer but also some of the new skills and competencies both of these roles required.

There are four core learning needs for today's health care trainers:

1. *Training and development.* Health care trainers need the skills of training development and design. These include assessing needs, creating learning objectives, designing interactive training modules, conducting material development, enhancing presentation and facilitation skills, and evaluating training.

2. *Health care acumen.* Health care is a complex industry. Health care trainers need to understand basic concepts of managed care, reimbursement, care delivery, and the core business of the organization. Health care leaders want to know that their trainers understand the difficulty of the world in which they live and work. They want trainers who can find solutions that result in changed performance.

3. *Consulting skills.* Both Roxanne and Sam function as training consultants. They work with employees and managers as consultants, identifying training solutions that best meet their needs. Their consulting skills include how to contract with the client, how to analyze needs, and how to intervene.

4. *Interpersonal skills.* A successful trainer is well skilled in the ability to communicate. Interpersonal skills include listening, confronting, influencing, and negotiating.

5. *Continuous learning.* A successful trainer is also a continuous learner. He is well schooled not just in health care but also in the areas in which he designs training. In addition, he seeks out professional development opportunities such as conferences, professional associations, and reading journals and books.

CONCLUSION

In this chapter, we have looked at how health care organizations typically set up their training departments in response to the trends and needs of their organizations. We then looked at how JCAHO influences the training department's focus and structure. We discussed the roles, responsibilities, and learning needs of the training professional in health care—the clinical educator and the employee and management development training specialist.

In the next chapters, we move to the how-to of designing and delivering training. We begin by looking at the key to successful training: assessing needs to ensure the right focus for training.

How to Do a
Needs Assessment

Picture a physician prescribing a course of treatment before first diagnosing the patient's illness. Hard to imagine, right? Yet, every day trainers do precisely that. They prescribe training as a treatment for problems before first understanding what the real problem is and the causes of the problem. Physicians use the tool of diagnosis and assessment to understand the symptoms of the illness before prescribing a treatment. The same approach is needed by trainers.

To diagnosis required training needs, trainers use a system called a *needs assessment*. In this chapter, we discuss how to develop and conduct a needs assessment. In particular, we focus on the components of a needs assessment: determining the sources of data, how to construct the actual assessment, methods for collecting data, how to analyze the data, and the components of the needs assessment report.

The chapter closes with a look at competencies, a key tool in health care for assessing and determining training needs. We look primarily at how competencies are used in health care, how competencies are developed, how competencies and training planning are done, and how to assess competence.

THE NEEDS ASSESSMENT

Needs assessment is a process to identify a performance problem and define the reason there is a gap between the desired behavior of the trainee and her actual performance (for example, knowing proper insertion of an IV into a patient versus actual performance in which the trainee misses the vein). The needs assessment helps to determine the causes of the incorrect performance and assesses if training is the best solution. It provides data to measure the impact or outcomes of the training, and it determines the priorities for training. Lastly, it can help to ensure that resources are spent appropriately.

Though the actual format may vary, the steps or process for conducting a needs assessment remains the same. It is similar to the process health care providers use in treating patients. The health care model for treating patients is:

- Assessment: What are the presenting problems?

- Diagnosis: Where does it hurt? (This includes examination and testing.)

- Treatment: applying treatment for the condition or issue, surgery, or medicine.

- Evaluation: Did the treatment work? Is the patient's condition improved?

Let's take a look at this model in action. A person comes into the physician's office complaining of mild indigestion and heartburn. The physician asks a series of questions about the patient's symptoms and orders some diagnostic tests, say, EKG and chest X ray. After all the results are returned and analyzed, she determines that the patient has a heart condition, not the presenting symptom of heartburn. She then devises a treatment plan that addresses the heart problem.

Developing a needs assessment resembles the treatment process. Using a similar path of having the trainer assess, diagnose, and then prescribe training, the needs assessment steps are:

1. Define the problem.

2. Determine the sources of data.

3. Construct the assessment (the diagnostic test).

4. Collect the data.

5. Analyze the data.

6. Develop the final report.

Define the Problem

The first step in developing a needs assessment is determining the focus of the assessment. It is important to understand what is actually happening and what should be happening. This involves developing a *gap analysis,* which helps to define what behaviors you see now and what behaviors you want to see in the future. For example, suppose a hospital's patient business services department requests training on telephone skills. Currently, patients are complaining that patient billing clerks are rude on the phone and calls are not returned for more than a week. The actual behaviors are poor phone etiquette and lack of timely response to patient questions. The desired behavior is for staff to use phrases such as "How can I help you?" or "I'm sorry for the inconvenience" and to respond to patient inquiries within twenty-four hours.

The gap analysis is a process wherein the trainer investigates the causes of the poor phone behavior. Is it due to lack of skill, or understaffing of the department, or poor resources? Once the causes of the gap between actual and desired performance are determined, then the trainer can suggest appropriate intervention methods, one of which may be training. This is a gap analysis.

Determine Sources of Data

After defining the problem and conducting a gap analysis to compare current behavior to the desired results, we now turn our attention to the next step: determining sources of data. Data are used to give the trainer information about not only the causes of the problem but also the effect on the individual and the organization.

Data also serve a role in the gap analysis process, primarily in determining the desired behavior. In the patient business services example, ascertaining the desired behavior concerning phone etiquette (appropriate phrases) comes from interviews and discussions with patients and managers. By defining the desired state, the sources of data become clear.

There are many sources of data available for the trainer to use in the needs assessment. They include the organization's employees, organizational information, and health care data.

Through an *employee interview* process, the trainer is able to determine the cause of the problem and the effect on a person's performance. A trainer may wish to interview senior managers, middle managers, the employees themselves, or other departments' employees to get information pertaining to possible causes of the performance problem. Before approaching employees, the trainer should consider who is closest to the problem, who is critical to performance success, and who can offer other perspectives. Each group can add a different insight to the actual needs assessment.

The second category of data, *organizational information,* includes the organization's strategic plan. This affords insight into the organization's direction and is often invaluable in determining future decisions. Other sources of information include the organization's mission statement, policies and procedures, surveys, customer satisfaction, employee satisfaction, quality reports, sources of errors, rework statistics, common complaints, rates of errors, job descriptions, exit interviews, and performance-evaluation summaries.

Third are *health care data.* Clinical quality reports (medication errors, falls, hospital infection rates, wait times), patient satisfaction data (in-house health care surveys and JCAHO survey scores), and risk management reports can all be invaluable in determining and supporting the need for training. Let's study a common example of analyzing data to design training by way of a trainer's perspective.

The trainer (let's call her Jean) has been asked to develop a training program for improving patient satisfaction, to ensure that the training program meets its objective of increased patient satisfaction. She takes a look at various forms of data. She reviews the patient satisfaction reports, which the hospital receives from recently discharged patients. She also reviews recent patient complaints. This information points to key issues in patient satisfaction: employees not introducing themselves when they enter a patient's room, not explaining tests and procedures, and not adequately responding to patient needs and issues.

To get an organizational perspective, Jean also looks at the hospital's vision, mission, and values, as well as strategic plans. These documents discuss patient satisfaction as a number one priority for the success of the system. Lastly, Jean refers to employee job descriptions to see if patient service expectations have been discussed.

As you can see in this example, by reviewing various sources of data Jean is better able to design a training program that actually achieves results. She can focus the training on the key drivers of patient satisfaction, as opposed to making assumptions about what patients want. This illustrates the value of investing in the needs assessment process.

Collect Data

After identifying the sources and kinds of data available, we now turn our attention to methods of collecting this kind of information. Selecting the most appropriate method is simple: What makes sense for the given project? Questions to consider are, What is simple to use? What makes the most sense based on the type and kind of information available? What provides the trainer with the specifics to design an effective strategy?

Methods are almost as varied as the sources of data: interviews, focus groups, surveys, observations, tests, and document review.

Interviews. Whether they are done in person or on the phone, interviews are a rich source of data. They can be time consuming, but with careful planning the benefits outweigh the costs.

To make interviews work, it is best to plan the questions in advance. They should be open-ended (that is, they cannot be answered with a yes or no) and framed with words such as *how, what,* or *why.* Although questions may vary with the focus of the assessment, here are some typical ones:

- How do you see the problem?
- In what particular situations do you see the performance problem, or is it a constant problem?
- What is happening today that may contribute to or cause the current performance problem?
- What performance would you like to see?

- What are the barriers or obstacles to performance?
- What are the skills, knowledge, and abilities that are needed to perform better?
- How would training help?

As part of the interview, begin by stating up front what the information is to be used for, or the purpose of the interview. It might be helpful to send the questions out in advance. In addition, clarifying the purpose may help to put the interviewee at ease. Many times he or she is concerned about confidentiality of responses. By addressing these concerns up front, it may help the interviewee feel more comfortable.

In addition to using open-ended questions, you may want to probe for specifics. Ask for particular examples or incidents that may help to explain situations. In addition, specifics can also become rich sources of information for training program materials, such as case studies and exercises.

Interviews produce qualitative rather than quantitative data. But they allow the interviewee to be part of the training process, and this may lead to increased support for the initiative. To help organize the information, consider an interview guide. It lists all of the questions and constitutes a means of organizing the information. Consider an interview guide used to develop a training program on communication skills.

1. Define *good communication skills* for me.
2. How effective is your team's use of good communication skills? Using a rating of 1 to 10, with 10 being the highest, what rating would you give your team?
3. How do good communication skills (or lack of same) affect the team's interpersonal relationships? Its team effectiveness?
4. What are typical interpersonal issues existing within your department?
5. How is conflict managed within the group?
6. If the team is performing effectively, describe the interpersonal relationships among team members.
7. If we could do one thing or focus on one skill to improve the effectiveness of the team, what would it be?

Focus Groups. A focus group is a meeting of participants who share a common specialty or field. Using a series of open-ended questions, the members of the focus groups build on one another's responses to give insight into specific questions. Focus groups allow the trainer to reach large groups of participants and generate considerable qualitative information that can be useful in identifying themes and gaining insight for your training programs.

Focus groups can also be hard to manage. It takes much skill at facilitation to keep participants on track. Keep the questions to a minimum (about five to seven), and set ground rules for the discussion. The main benefit of a focus group is that it saves time.

Surveys. Surveys are easy to construct and administer. They are especially helpful when employees work in more than one location. The biggest drawback is the return rate, which is typically low. Another drawback is interpretation. Since communication is limited to what is presented on the printed page, it can be difficult to interpret the responses.

There are several approaches to constructing a survey. One is to use open-ended questions, similar to an interview. Multiple choice ("Check the response that applies"), rating scale ("Rank the importance of this skill to your development as a manager on a scale of 1 to 7"), or rank order ("Rank these skills in order of importance for effectively communicating with patients") are other survey options.

One form of survey that I have found to be particularly helpful does two assessments, as you will note in Exhibit 3.1. Here the respondees rate each skill for its importance to the role of a nurse manager and also whether it is a development need. In this assessment, you can prioritize not only key skills for a position but also the critical development needs of the nurse managers.

It is important to keep some simple guidelines in mind when creating surveys or questionnaires. Write clear instructions ("Please read the following tasks, and circle the word that best describes how often you perform the task: frequently, rarely, never"). Write the survey items clearly and logically. Select an appropriate format for the survey. Leave space for comments, and note when the survey needs to be returned. You might also want to include some demographics as part of the questionnaire: length of employment, unit, and job class. You may want someone to pilot the questionnaire to help get the bugs out prior to mailing it. Send out a cover letter with the survey that explains the purpose of the survey and how the data are to be used. Although paper-and-pencil interviews are the easiest, it is now possible to conduct this type of survey through e-mail or a website.

**Exhibit 3.1 Educational Needs Assessment for
Nursing Administrative Supervisory Group**

Introduction

This survey is designed to get your ideas about the developmental needs of the Nursing Administrative Supervisory Group. The information will be used only to develop a curriculum that specifically meets the needs of this leadership team. Your answers are completely confidential and will be processed only for the entire group. Please return the completed survey to XXXXX.

Part 1: Survey Directions

For each of the skills below:

1. Please circle one number in the first column to indicate how important you think the skill is to successful performance of your job.

2. Then circle one number in the second column to indicate your need for further development of this skill.

Skill	Importance to the Job					Development Need for Me				
	Low				High	Low				High
Coaching and counseling (communicates performance expectations, provides constructive feedback, focuses on performance problems, sets action plan for improvement)	1	2	3	4	5	1	2	3	4	5
Delegation (relieves self of duties through appropriate assignment of work, sets realistic deadlines, follows up on assignments)	1	2	3	4	5	1	2	3	4	5

Observation. Observation can be used to objectively assess the environment in which the performance takes place, the steps in a task, or skills. As a new trainer, I often used observations when I was unfamiliar with the work environment or the job duties. For example, I was once asked to develop an interviewing skills program for medical residents. To better equip myself with the right examples, I spent time with residents, observing them interview patients. This experience revealed skills and behaviors that I have since incorporated into my training designs.

When using the observation approach, keep in mind a few practical suggestions:

- Carefully explain the purpose of your observation to the employees.

- Remain neutral. Avoid coaching or advising; instead, try to remain unobtrusive.

- Document the activity carefully. You might want to create a worksheet or time log. Use specifics to describe the activities.

- Observations are time consuming. Devote an appropriate amount of time to observing the entire task.

Tests. In health care, there are several proficiency or competency tests that trainers can use as part of a needs assessment. Some of the tests you may come across include phlebotomy skills, Accucheck, and medication administration. In my organization, nurses are tested in such areas as pharmacy dosage calculations, reading EKGs, and CPR. Reviewing these types of tests for common errors may help a trainer determine where to focus skill development. For example, when reviewing the EKG exams, it helps to identify what type of rhythm strip gives the nurses the most trouble so that training can focus on that element.

Document Reviews. Just as a doctor on rounds reviews charts to see the treatment plan for his patients, or to change medications, so do trainers use documents. As we discussed earlier, there are several sources of data available for the trainer to review. These include patient and customer satisfaction information, policies and procedures, and work samples. Document reviews are often used to support other information. If managers identify customer-service skills, a review of existing patient and customer information may support the skills identified and again help to focus the trainer on the area of greatest need. In addition, reviewing documents may elicit organizational background information and a historical perspective.

As a trainer, I find document reviews a key needs assessment strategy. This review is a critical part of linking training to the business goals of the organization.

Recently, business planning was identified as a need for managers within my organization. To help design the program, I reviewed the strategic planning process. This review gave me the specifics of what had to be included in business planning, as well as how the business plans should link to the strategic planning process. Document reviews are easy to do and require few resources. The biggest factor is usually accessing the information and identifying trends and patterns.

In summary, these are the most common approaches to collecting needs assessment data (Table 3.1). Surveys, focus groups, interviews, and observations can all be used to build effective training designs.

Analyzing the Information

After the information is collected, the most crucial step in the needs assessment process is analysis. It can be as simple as reviewing the data and looking for common themes or issues, or as complex as statistical analysis. Either way, the analysis should, if possible, tie directly into the method used. If the method produces qualitative data (interviews, focus groups, observations), a thematic analysis is effective. The thematic method involves summarizing all the data according to question and then determining the common themes. For example, a theme may concern the ability of the employees to handle conflict, which would help to

Table 3.1 A Comparison of Needs Assessment Methods

Method	Pros	Cons
Interviews	Can clarify information immediately Can ask questions Can follow up with additional information	Time consuming Subjective information; hard to quantify
Focus groups	Can reach large groups of people Can generate large sums of data	Subjective information Might intimidate participants Can be hard to manage
Surveys or questionnaires	Easy to administer Quick and time-efficient Able to reach large numbers of people	Low response rate Possibly difficult to interpret
Observation	Able to see job in action	Time intensive Difficult to assess

focus a communication skills program on confrontation skills. This aids trending the information; therefore, the trainer can focus on the most important skills as identified by the majority of the interviewees, rather than react to data that are important to only one or two interviewees.

For those methods that produce objective information or quantitative data, use averages, medians and means, and percentages in the analysis. This method often works best with surveys ("Twenty-five people responded that listening was a key development need for managers"). Again, this mathematical analysis helps to differentiate actual needs from assumptions.

Developing the Final Report

After conducting the analysis, the trainer is well on her way to determining the best course of action. If training is called for, it helps to determine the length and training content as well as specifics for learning activities. In a needs assessment looking at communication skills, the data may yield insights to specific content areas such as conflict management, listening, and feedback. In addition, the data might give the trainer facts that are helpful in writing a case study.

How are training and learning needs determined? This is a favorite question of health care regulatory agencies such as JCAHO. Normally as part of the accreditation process, there is an interview with the education department about learning needs and how these needs are linked to the education plan. Documenting needs is a good habit for every trainer. It shows connection between skills, forms the basis for measuring results, and systematically defines training in the context of resolving performance problems. Normally, the needs assessment is documented in a final report. The report can be as simple as a chart or graph, or as complex as a written narrative. What matters is that the trainer document how needs were assessed and what the specific results were. The final report should include the four major components outlined in the next paragraphs.

The Executive Overview. This overview is simply a one-or-two-page summary of the findings of the needs analysis and the recommended course of action.

Description of the Process. This includes a statement of the problem or need, sources of data, who was involved in the analysis, and methods used to collect information.

Data Collection Summary. Included in this section are demographics of the people involved, a graphical representation of the analysis of the data (table or chart), and samples of any instruments.

Recommended Course of Action. This should include the proposed interventions, time lines, and costs. Typically, I use this final report format to introduce new programs or processes for any major initiative. For example, I used this report to illustrate how I developed my organization's leadership development curriculum. The report identified the type of skills needed and how training would address those needs.

For a needs analysis that is done to determine content of a training program, I do a modified report that includes a summary of the data and recommendations.

SAMPLE NEEDS ASSESSMENTS

I include two examples of needs assessment as addenda to this chapter; they illustrate ways of collecting and analyzing results. The first, a management development questionnaire, is a survey instrument; it identifies developmental needs. It uses a rating system as well as open-ended questions. This survey was used to garner information for developing a management and executive curriculum. I myself use this questionnaire annually to assist in planning the year's leadership and management development programs. This tool is simple to use and gives me the development needs for each skill area.

The second, a clinical needs questionnaire, was designed to identify what types of clinical training are required. As a questionnaire, it uses both a rating scale for learning need and importance and open-ended questions. These allow the respondee to offer more information than a simple number affords. Like the first assessment, this survey includes an introduction that states why it is being done and what will happen to the information.

NEEDS ASSESSMENT CASE STUDY

Ed is the manager of a respiratory therapy department. He has requested that Cheryl, a training specialist, conduct customer-service training for his staff because they have been missing treatments for patients and he has received several complaints. Before committing to teach customer service, Cheryl and Ed have agreed to conduct a needs assessment to determine whether training is the best approach.

The first step is for Cheryl to spend time determining what "customer service" means to Ed and his staff. Cheryl also wants to determine what "missed treatments" are.

Ed defined customer service as delivering the right treatment to the right patient at the right time. In further discussions, he identified missed treatments as meaning that the therapist does not deliver the treatment to the patient on time, and that this problem occurs with all staff members.

As the second step, Cheryl needs to determine sources of data available. They might include patient satisfaction data, observations of staff, interviews with staff and nursing personnel, statistical reports of missed treatments, and demographics of the employees in respiratory (for instance, how long have these employees worked in respiratory? are they new to the field? etc.). Some of the data collected are:

- Missed treatment reports that show there were twenty missed treatments in each of the last three months. Of the twenty missed treatments, twelve were missed entirely, and the rest were delivered more than two hours behind schedule. The missed treatments occurred on the medicine and surgical units, primarily during the day shift.

- Patient satisfaction, showing that patients rated timeliness of respiratory treatment as 3.5 on a 5-point scale.

- Employee tally: there are fifteen therapists, five of whom are new to the department, having recently graduated from a therapist program.

In the third step, Cheryl decides to use a variety of approaches in collecting data. She decides to interview all the staff members individually, as well as selected nursing personnel in the nursing units involved.

Questions she will ask include:

- What does *customer service* mean to you?

- Describe your typical day.

- What gets in the way of meeting your treatment schedule? (Lack of resources, scheduling, lack of communication, etc.)

- Describe a typical interaction with a patient.

- What training would help you improve your ability to provide excellent customer service to your patients?

Cheryl is also going to follow three therapists to observe directly what a typical day is like.

Fourth, here is a summary of the information Cheryl has collected:

1. What does *customer service* mean to you?
   - Customer service is providing our patients with good-quality care.
   - Giving treatments on time and correctly.
   - Treating our patients with respect.

2. Describe your typical day.
   - I give about thirty-five treatments a day. They're spread all over the hospital. I'm always on the go.
   - I get the list of scheduled treatments when I come in and then I start to deliver them.
   - I get beeped about ten times during the day for stat treatments and unscheduled treatment; sometimes that puts me behind on the schedule.

3. What gets in the way of meeting your treatment schedule?
   - The unscheduled treatment causes me to miss scheduled ones sometimes.
   - Sometimes I have to wait because a patient is not ready; they might be eating their breakfast, or they are not in their room.
   - I have to run between three and four units on three floors; it takes time getting the equipment to the right unit.

4. Describe a typical interaction with a patient.
   - Most patients are fine.
   - Some patients don't understand what a treatment is and what I'm doing; it takes time to explain the treatment to them.

5. What training would help you improve your ability to provide excellent customer service to your patients?
   - Listening skills
   - Stress management
   - How to explain information

6. From the nursing unit interviews, Cheryl receives this information:

- Respiratory therapists are often late, which means that we're late getting the patients to other tests and treatments.
- The respiratory therapists are not prepared and often have to ask who's receiving the treatment, etc.

7. From the observations with the three therapists, Cheryl develops this time log:

- 7:30: respiratory therapist receives assignment for the day (thirty-five treatments).
- 7:35: gathers supplies and begins treatment.
- 7:50: waits at elevator and talks with other therapists.
- 8:05: arrives on unit and stops at nursing unit to find out the patient's room number.

The fifth step in this case-study needs assessment is to review the information. Doing so, Cheryl determines a course of action. She realizes that customer-service training is not the best solution to this problem at this time. Consequently, Cheryl and Ed determine that one of the initial ways to resolve this issue is to schedule patients better, and to group patients by floor. Ed also organizes an on-call therapist to respond to the unscheduled treatments. Next, Ed works with the nursing units to give the therapist specific information on the patients, to better organize their assignments prior to going to the floor. After these solutions are implemented, Cheryl might consider training in the area of organizing patient assignment and time management.

In this example, the trainer will probably continue to work with the manager using a combination of facilitation and analysis skills. The trainer might work to flowchart the patient scheduling process and determine where the system is flawed. In addition, the trainer might continue to coach the manager on how to deal with these issues through performance management with the employee.

COMPETENCIES AND TRAINING

A single unifying theme for health care training practitioners is competence assessments. Competency assessment forms the basis of performance improvement in health care. Most regulatory agencies require competency assessment to ensure that the care delivered to patients meets a required quality level. In this section, we look at competency assessments, what they are, how they are developed, and how they are used in the health care setting.

WHAT IS COMPETENCE?

In health care today, competence plays a crucial role. Given constant change in technology, restructuring, and regulatory requirements, it is essential that employees adequately perform their jobs. Most health care organizations measure employee performance through competencies, which are usually made up of a statement that identifies the skills along with the specific behaviors necessary to perform the skill. In addition to the skills and behaviors, there is often an indication of how the competency is validated or tested.

As I mentioned earlier in this book, today's health care professionals require new clinical and nonclinical skill sets. Let's first look at clinical skill sets. Nurses, for example, are required to assess patients, develop patient care plans, and manage patient care. Each component requires a host of skills. Managing patient care, depending on the specialty, can require such skills as chest tube management, postoperative care, wound care, and intravenous drug management.

Other providers, such as physical therapists and respiratory therapists, require a different set of skills. Physical therapists must do functional assessments as well as perform physical therapy treatments, and manage patients requiring orthopedics and cardiac rehabilitation. Respiratory therapists need to understand airway management, ventilation management, and intubation. As the examples in Table 3.2 show, each profession has a unique set of skills that define the profession.

In addition to clinical skills, there are also a host of nonclinical skills that all health care employees must be aware of. These include compliance with fire and safety regulations, infection control procedures, and communication and customer service skills (and for some others, training and supervisory skills). With this wide variation in skill requirements, it is essential that managers and staff understand the skills they are expected to perform. These performance expectations often form the basis of a competency. Typically, a competency is the set of skills that must be performed adequately in order to be successful. This is illustrated by the example in Exhibit 3.2.

Table 3.2 Sample Skill (Competency) Requirements

Profession	Competency
Nursing	Blood glucose monitoring Cardiac rhythm identification Patient assessment
Conscious sedation	Central venous catheter Peritoneal dialysis
Emergency room	Age-specific care Thrombolytic therapy
Pharmacy	IV preparation Pharmaceutical calculations Chemotherapy compounding
Dietitian	Dietary needs, appropriate to disease and age Calculating calories and portions
Respiratory therapy	Bronchodilator administration Mini-nebulizer treatment Avian bird ventilation Arterial blood gases

USING COMPETENCIES

Competencies have many uses in health care. They are a means of ensuring that a new employee understands what is expected and is properly trained to fulfill these expectations. For example, in my organization, one of our competencies for employees is recognizing the signs of abuse. In this competency, we explain how employees should assess abuse among patients and follow the organizational policy for reporting this abuse.

Competencies can be tied to ongoing educational planning, thus forming the basis for continuous skill development. With the example of our abuse competency, we know that all employees need to be competent in this area. Therefore, as we plan our training programs for the year, we have to offer adequate training sessions in this area.

In addition, competencies are being integrated into other human resource systems of selection and evaluation. In selection, for example, competencies can be used to help define what a successful nurse manager may look like. The competencies can then be translated into selection criteria and questions for use in

Exhibit 3.2 Sample Competency for Phlebotomy

Employee name: _____ Title: _____

Division/unit: _____ Date: _____

(Check one) Initial review: ❏   Three-month review: ❏   Annual review: ❏

Performance Criteria	Satisfactory	Unsatisfactory	Comments

1. Identification
 	
    A. Identification bracelets
       • Importance of checking
       • Action if patient is without one			

B. IV lines and heparin locks (if applicable)			

2. Procedure
 	
    A. Introduce self to patient
       and describe procedure			

B. Check identification bracelet			
C. Prepare venipuncture site			

determining the best candidate for a position. In this example, you can see how the competencies for the nurse manager are woven into selection questions:

Selection Questions for Nurse Manager

Nurse manager's competencies were identified as

- Customer-service focus

- Judgment and ability to solve problems

- Ability to manage stress; flexibility

1. Selection questions: customer-service focus

   - Describe a time when you handled a difficult patient complaint. How did you involve others in resolving this issue?

   - Describe the process you use to engage physicians in the operation of your unit.

2. Selection questions: judgment and problem solving

- Give an example of a problem you had to resolve under a tight deadline. What did you do to meet the deadline?

- What was a tough decision you had to make? What process did you follow?

Competencies can also be tied to succession planning. Succession planning is the process of determining future capabilities and talents for key positions, and determining methods to prepare those of high potential for promotion and growth. The process normally entails first determining what executive or managerial succession is needed, based on the strategic and organizational plan.

Next, the organization determines what type of competencies are required in these positions, as well as assessing where and how the competencies now exist. After review of the talent, the next step is to determine what kind of competency development programs are needed. In most cases, succession planning ties directly to management development by creating development programs that align with current and future organizational needs.

Competencies can also be tied to the performance review process. This can be accomplished through including competencies and expectations in every employee's job description and evaluation.

In addition, as part of the review, there is an opportunity to generate purposeful dialogue on development. An individualized development plan, or IDP, is often created based on the competencies, to provide a framework for that year's personal and professional development. Included in the IDP are discussion of goals and objectives, key performance goals, and a plan for accomplishing them. Exhibit 3.3 is a sample of an individualized learning plan.

Competencies can be made even stronger by linking them to the human resource systems of selection, succession planning, and performance management. These systems are the natural backdrop for reinforcing effective performance. By ensuring that the right employee is selected for the right position, by creating a process for evaluating their performance and identifying future talent, the process for development is strengthened and rewarded.

One of the latest trends is developing management competencies. Because many clinicians are promoted to management positions on the basis of their technical expertise—often with little regard for their management abilities—the competencies of this role must be clarified. I have found this to be a useful process for

Exhibit 3.3 Sample Individual Learning Plan

The Individual Learning Profile is designed to help you plan your personal and professional development. The plan will help you and your manager identify and create developmental opportunities. After you have completed the plan, please discuss it with your manager.

Name: _____ Title: _____

Department: _____ Period: _____

Manager's signature: _____

1. Creating your personal and professional profile:
   - What are your strengths, interests, and areas of proficiency? _____
     _____
   - Areas of potential growth? _____
     _____
   - What is your logical career path? _____
     _____

2. Identify:
   - Long-range (3–5 years) individual development goal
   - Short-term (1–2 years) individual development goal

Developmental Plan

3. Identify activities that you will engage in over the next year or two.

Activity	Topic or focus	Funding requirements	When	Ways to evaluate effectiveness
(course assignment, training, personal wellness, sabbatical, professional conference, individual project) 1. 2. 3. 4.				

managers. First, it identifies what successful management might look like, and second, it helps to plan the type of learning program for managers. Here is an illustration of what management competencies look like:

Sample Management Competencies

1. Dealing with ambiguity

- Coping effectively with change

- Shifting gears comfortably

- Deciding and acting without the total picture

2. Business knowledge

- Knowing how businesses work

- Knowledgeable in current and future policies, practices, trends, and information affecting his or her business and organization

DEVELOPING COMPETENCIES

In many ways, JCAHO drives the competency practices of today's health care organizations. As we saw in Chapter Two, JCAHO expects the organization to develop and assess competencies in several key areas (such as fire safety, patient confidentiality, advance directives, etc.).

In addition to the regulatory competencies, organizations also have to develop competencies. This involves three steps:

1. Analyzing the job

2. Comparing the requirements of current and future competencies

3. Identifying the skills and behaviors that apply

For example, after analyzing the job of a nurse manager, we determine that they must be able to develop a staffing plan that adequately staffs their unit. After comparing their current job duties against the standard of developing a staffing plan, the trainer then determines that the requisite skills include analytical thinking, judgment, and critical thinking. These skills form the basis of the staffing planning process—which might be a competency for the nurse manager position.

Competencies work best when validated or tested by employees who are currently in the position and who meet or exceed the job requirements. These exceptional performers not only help determine the job expectations but also know best how to perform the actual job. In our nurse manager example, exceptional performers identify how to develop the plan and the steps in the planning process. They help determine the content of the competency and then validate or test to see if the competency actually works.

Another way competencies are developed is by using a formula (we do this in our organization). This method looks at practices and procedures and identifies the frequency of use, as well as the critical nature of the issue. We then develop competencies based on skills that are used infrequently but have critical importance.

For example, if a nurse only has to insert a catheter in a central line two to three times a year but failure to perform this task properly can cause an adverse patient outcome, then we would write a competency. The premise is that those activities that are done frequently result in greater opportunities to practice and remain current.

After the competencies are developed, trainers need to know how to develop training that supports the organization's competencies. For example, if understanding the business of health care is one of the competencies in an organization, the training staff would develop a learning experience that teaches managers the basic business aspects of the health care industry. Depending on the skills and behaviors required, this probably includes how to read financial reports, discuss how managed care works, and explain how the hospital makes money. These competencies should form the basis of a *training plan*. The plan includes a description of how training is conducted, as well as how it ties into each competency.

One way to maximize competency training and development is to create a standardized format for organizational competency plans. This helps any department or individual make sure that the competencies being developed meet organizational standards.

ASSESSING COMPETENCE

Next to developing competencies, the most important function of health care training is assessing competence. There are several ways to do so, primarily through testing, observation, and demonstration.

Testing

The employee completes a test that shows his knowledge level in a key area of competence. Testing is used in clinical competencies, such as medication administration and fire safety. In both of these cases, a test is designed that focuses on the key components of the competency. A baseline level—a number or percentage of correct answers—also helps to ensure employee competence.

Sample Phlebotomy Test Questions

1. When performing a venipuncture, what is the most important aspect in the phlebotomy procedure?

A. Patient identification

B. Handwashing

C. Applying gloves

2. When performing a venipuncture, what is the order of draw?

A. Purple, red, blue, yellow

B. Red, blue, purple, yellow

C. Yellow, red, blue, purple

When using testing, JCAHO often requires that a certain percentage of the employees be able to successfully complete the test on these competencies. These figures are required for hospital boards.

Observation

A staff member can verify competence by observing another staff member performing the actual job. Observation works well because it can be used in actual work settings; it thus replicates the environment in which the job or task is performed. Observation can be subjective, unless there are specific task standards that the employees must meet. It tends to work better for nonclinical competencies. In a competency that focuses on customer service, observing an employee attending to a customer is a valid way to assess the employee's competence.

Demonstration

In this method, the employee demonstrates an actual job skill for another employee. As with observation, demonstration tends to be subjective in nature. An example of demonstrating competence is cardiopulmonary resuscitation. In CPR, the employee demonstrates how to perform this technique.

RECORDING COMPETENCIES

JCAHO requires strict record keeping for competencies. These records include the competency, the method of validation, and a score if applicable. In some cases, the actual tests or validation instruments may also need to be indicated. These records are often part of an educational file or employee personnel file. Another important record is the orientation competency record, which registers the competencies required for new employees. It serves as a plan for new employees to learn about important aspects of a job.

CONCLUSION

In this chapter we have discussed the basics of how to develop and conduct a needs assessment. In particular, we identified the components of a needs assessment: determining the sources of data, how to construct the actual assessment, methods for collecting data, how to analyze the data, and the components of the needs assessment report.

We then moved our discussion to the role of competence as a tool of needs assessment and planning in a health care organization. We looked primarily at how competencies are used in health care, how they are developed, and how competency and training planning are done, as well as the most significant ways competencies are assessed. As we move into the training design as the focus for the next chapter, we see how needs assessments are used in preparing and designing training programs.

ADDENDUM ONE
TRAINING AND EDUCATION NEEDS ASSESSMENT FOR MANAGERS

Introduction

This survey is designed to elicit your feedback about your training and education needs as a member of the management team. The information will be used to determine course offerings for 1998. Your answers are completely confidential, and results will be analyzed for each organizational or management level. Please return the completed survey to _____.

PART I

Please select one answer to indicate your need for further skill development: low, medium, or high.

Skill Development Area	Low Need	Medium Need	High Need
1. Coaching and counseling: I communicate performance expectations, provide productive feedback, focus on performance problems, and set action plans for improvement.			
2. Recognition: I value employee contributions, recognize employees' efforts, give clear direction, and spark others into action.			
3. Financial management: I measure, monitor, and evaluate department performance against objectives; manage financial statements to meet departmental goals; know how to develop and analyze budget plans; and can read and interpret financial statements.			
4. Collaboration: I collaborate with departments, solicit input and feedback regarding process improvement, encourage partnerships with internal and external customers, and build relationships.			
5. Time management: I manage time well, set priorities, meet deadlines, set goals, and follow through in an organized manner.			
6. Oral and written communication: I make points effectively when presenting ideas to others and write clear and grammatically correct memos, letters, and reports.			
7. Customer-focused: I listen to customers; spend time visibly interacting with patients, visitors, and colleagues; and effectively consolidate and act upon customer feedback.			

Skill Development Area	Low Need	Medium Need	High Need
8. Change management: I introduce needed changes in my department, understand the change process, and help employees understand; I constantly search for ways to do things better and encourage others to find better ways of doing things.			
9. Risk taking: I seize new opportunities, do not punish people who make mistakes, and constantly generate new ideas.			
10. Decision making: I solicit input from others, involve the right people, reach decisions after considering other points of view, communicate the decisions that have been made, implement decisions, and don't procrastinate.			
11. Relationship building: I encourage feedback and open communication, can relate to different types of people, build cooperative relationships, and trust others to do their best.			
12. Problem solving: I use internal and external information to identify and evaluate alternative solutions to situations.			
13. Planning: I use internal and external information to develop action plans, translate plans into action, monitor and evaluate outcomes, and effectively organize and manage long-term assignments.			
14. Delegation: I relieve myself of duties through appropriate assignment of work, set realistic deadlines, and follow up on assignments.			
15. Individual performance planning with employees: I recognize employee potential, recommend and offer training opportunities, and reinforce training with follow-up meetings.			
16. Conflict management: I confront others skillfully, can resolve differences effectively, and can negotiate agreements.			
17. Productive meetings: I identify and clarify the outcomes that meetings are intended to accomplish, set standards/ guidelines to be followed during meetings, use agendas to conduct department meetings, and evaluate the effectiveness of department meetings.			

Skill Development Area	Low Need	Medium Need	High Need
18. Diversity: I value differences between people, respect people's different backgrounds, value and draw from the work experiences people bring, and value the culture, beliefs, and practices of others.			
19. Team development: I know how groups develop and evolve, and can pinpoint team problems and fix them effectively. I know how to show support and consideration of others, how to focus on the task and get the job done.			
20. Human resources: I know how to select employees, understand the Human Resources policies and procedures, understand the disciplinary process, and am familiar with the union contracts, pay practices, and the legal aspects of personnel relations including interviewing and selection.			
21. Teamwork: I build commitment to new ideas, share authority with others, and influence others to take action.			
22. Strategic thinking: I consider internal and external factors when solving problems and making decisions; I ensure a fit between my department's actions and the organization's mission, vision, and values, and identify critical and high payoff strategies.			
23. Leadership: I foster a common vision and values, influence organization direction, and guide the department to accomplish goals consistent with the vision.			

PART II

Please comment on the questions below.

1. Think back to when you first started your present job. What type of management training would have helped you at that time? _____

_____

_____

2. What initiatives should the training department plan to better serve the management staff and help to improve the organization's overall effectiveness?

_____

_____

_____

3. What kind of training does your supervisory staff need?

- ❏ Performance management
- ❏ Communication
- ❏ Conflict management
- ❏ Teamwork
- ❏ Basic supervisory development
- ❏ Effective meetings
- ❏ Other (specify) _____

_____

ADDENDUM TWO
CLINICAL EDUCATION NEEDS ASSESSMENT

The Training Department is currently reviewing the programs offered to clinical staff. This is part of a continuing effort to update the training programs in response to needs perceived by system employees. The information collected will be used to develop clinical education programs.

Please assist us in this process by completing the attached survey and returning it to in the Training Department by (date) _____.

Department: _____ Division: _____

Job title: _____

1. Have you attended any training programs offered by the Organizational Effectiveness Department?   yes ❑   no ❑

2. If yes, which programs? _____

3. Was the training helpful to you in your present position?   yes ❑   no ❑

4. If yes, how was it helpful? If no, why not? _____

   _____

5. Have you received any on-the-job training specific to your current job from your supervisor or coworkers?   yes ❑   no ❑

6. If so, did the on-the-job training adequately prepare you to do your job?
   yes ❑   no ❑

7. If yes, how was it helpful? If no, why not? _____

   _____

8. What are the key changes occurring in health care that will have the greatest impact on the delivery of care that you provide? _____

   _____

9. Please rate the following topics on a scale of 1 to 3 in two categories: to what degree it is a learning need of yours (L), and the importance (I) of the skill in completing your job.

Learning Need

1 = no need

2 = moderate need

3 = great need

Importance

1 = low importance

2 = moderate importance

3 = great importance

L	I	Program Topic
		Advanced directives
		Advanced IV infusion
		Advanced med/surg
		Balancing work and home stresses
		Basic dysrhythmia
		Body mechanics
		Cardiac rhythm identification
		Code Blue response
		Conflict resolution
		Critical care
		Critical thinking
		Customer service
		Dealing with combative patients
		Dealing with death and dying
		Dealing with difficult patients and families
		Delegation

L	I	Program Topic
		Disease-specific education (e.g., hepatitis)
		Diversity in the workplace
		Effective communication
		Interpreting lab results
		Legal aspects of documentation
		Medical terminology
		Medication updates
		Mentor training
		Pain management
		Physical assessment
		Postorientation workshop
		Presentation skills
		Problem-solving strategies
		Team-building skills
		Time management
		Understanding diversity

10. In the past, clinical education has focused on nursing. Our focus has broadened to include ancillary departments, such as physical therapy, pharmacy, and radiology. What type of training would be beneficial to your department? _____

    _____

11. What type of training involving clinical skills would be beneficial to you?

    _____

    _____

12. What type of training involving use of equipment would be beneficial to you?

    _____

    _____

13. What type of training format would work best for your unit? (Check those that apply.)

    ❑ All day, eight-hour program

    ❑ Half-day, four-hour program

    ❑ Lunchtime, one-hour program

    ❑ Self-learning packets

    ❑ Computer-based training

14. What is the best time of day to offer training? _____

    _____

15. Where is the ideal place to hold the training? _____

    _____

16. Other suggestions or comments: _____

    _____

How to Design a Training Program

Now that we have looked at the process of determining training needs and competency, we turn to the steps for designing a training program.

As a trainer, I love the design portion of training. The design elements represent for me the meat and potatoes of training. What I mean by this is that designing allows you to actually see how learning comes to life; nothing is more exciting than creating a well-framed training design.

In this chapter we look at the process that I use in training design, from creating a purpose statement and objectives, to developing the content and methodology, to designing materials and evaluation methods. We also learn some creative ways to add energy and interest to training.

THE TRAINING DESIGN MODEL

Will's Training Design

Will, an employee development training specialist, is designing a training program on communication skills. After conducting a needs analysis and determining needs, he is ready to begin the training design process. He begins with identifying or stating the overall goals of the training program.

His program focuses on listening and giving feedback. After he determines the overall goals, he then creates the learning objectives, or what specifically the participants will learn as a result of attending the training program. These objectives form the basis for determining the learning content or what specialty he will cover in the training program, as well as how he will cover it.

For example, one of his objectives is that the participants be able to identify and use nonverbal cues of listening. Will has designed a short lecture for use in illustrating the points; he has created a small group activity that allows the participants to practice these nonverbal cues.

After he develops his learning methods, he prepares his program materials or participant workbook. He wraps up by determining how he will evaluate whether the program has met the objectives.

As you can see, Will employs a systematic approach to training design. The steps he uses are:

1. Create a statement of purpose.

2. Determine the learning objectives.

3. Design program content.

4. Determine learning methodologies.

5. Design program materials.

6. Determine evaluation methods.

Statement of Purpose

Step one in the design process is determining the overall purpose of the training program. The statement of purpose is a one- or two-sentence statement that is the basic understanding of what the training is being designed to achieve; it also delineates the scope of the training. For a training program on communication skills program, the purpose statement might be "To provide an overview of the basic components of interpersonal communication skills, including listening, conflict resolution, and feedback." The statement of purpose for a seminar on death and dying might be "To provide the participants with an understanding of the five stages of death and dying."

Normally the purpose statements include action verbs ("provide," "review," and so on). One way I use a purpose statement is to furnish the boundaries of the program. In the death and dying seminar, the purpose statement tells as much about what is not covered as it does about what is covered. In this seminar you would not, for instance, find grieving information, since it has not been included in the purpose.

Determine the Learning Objectives

After determining the statement of purpose, step two is to determine the learning objectives. Learning objectives are the foundation of determining what the results of attending the training program will be. Objectives are often overlooked; that is, many trainers try to design without them. Yet the most skilled designer knows that the core for an excellent program is development of learning objectives.

Objectives create focus and force the trainer to think about what the results of the training should be and how these results are achieved. Use your needs assessment information to determine which specific skills to focus on in the class. For example, in the aforementioned course on interpersonal skills, your objectives might be to practice listening skills, to learn a model for effective interpersonal communication, and to identify steps in a conflict-resolution process.

Effective learning objectives have three components:

1. The performance that is required

2. The condition of the performance

3. The criterion or criteria that describe the quality and quantity expected

Performance

The performance aspect of an objective must offer specifics on what the learner is able to do or how the learner performs. Performance should be observable and measurable; use verbs to indicate it.

Action verbs that help to indicate performance include:

Analyze	Assess
Evaluate	Prepare
Understand	Demonstrate
Design	Develop
Compare	Identify

Describe	List
Explain	Distinguish
Write	Speak

Condition

Condition implies the circumstances under which the performance takes place. It may include the tools, job aids, methods, or time involved in the performance. Condition plays an important role in clinical learning objectives. In many cases, special equipment must be used or special procedures followed. Spelling this out helps the learner clarify the performance expectations.

Criteria

Criteria are the yardstick for performance, the gauge by which quality and quantity are judged. The criteria for successful completion of the performance are stated in specific terms that can be measured or observed.

Examples

Here are examples of learning objectives for clinical and nonclinical programs:

- Managers will be able to prepare [performance] an error-free operating budget [criterion] using Microsoft Excel [condition].

- Using the American Heart Association's CPR methods [condition], the participant will be able to demonstrate [performance] the use of CPR on the Annie doll without an error [criteria].

- Participants will be able to recognize and interpret [performance] EKG rhythm strips on cardiac patients [conditions] without errors 100 percent of the time [criterion].

- At the end of the Coaching and Counseling workshop, the participant will be able to create an individualized development plan [performance] using Fournie's method [condition] 100 percent of the time [criterion].

In these examples, you can see how all of the components work together to create a specific and measurable learning objective. The learning objective is also an excellent way to measure the success of the training. It details not only the performance criteria but also those that can be used to evaluate achievement.

Design Program Content

After the objectives are developed, the next step in the process is to design the curriculum or lesson plan for the program. Normally, the design step includes developing a lesson plan, researching the content, organizing the content, and designing individual modules or lessons.

In preparing the program content, you must do some research on the subject matter. Researching for content may involve talking to individuals who successfully perform the job or skill, reading books and articles, or reviewing other programs or seminars. I find that research is a great opportunity to identify what should be included in the program content and often provides good examples of exercises that can be used to illustrate various points.

After the topic has been researched, it is time to begin organizing the content. There are various ways to do so. One can organize the material according to the natural progression of concepts (what information is needed prior to introducing the next bit of information); for example, in a presentation-skills training program, reviewing the various components of a successful presentation occurs prior to practicing presentation skills. Another method is to move from a general concept to specific principles; to take an example, in designing a program on conducting a performance appraisal, start by reviewing the purpose of the performance evaluation and the steps that make up an effective evaluation, and then move to specific tools for developing performance standards. Be logical and think through what would work best if you were the learner.

After determining the content and its organization, it is time to design individual lessons and create the lesson plan. Lessons or modules divide the training into specific categories. Lessons are often based on individual objectives and organized sequentially. Try starting with the desired result or goal and then work backwards.

Here is an example, developing a lesson on drawing blood.

Goal: Draw Blood

Step 4 ↔ Blood-drawing process

Step 3 ↔ How to operate equipment to draw blood

Step 2 ↔ How to locate a vein

Step 1 ↔ Basic anatomy

In this example, the lesson plan for drawing blood is organized sequentially. A sequential learning plan helps determine what skills and abilities participants may need to bring with them, and any prerequisites for the training. In this example, the lesson starts with basic anatomy. It might presuppose that the participants have some knowledge about anatomy and blood. The steps build upon each other.

After the lessons are developed, they are organized into a lesson plan. The lesson plan is the map or outline for the training program. It provides direction for the trainer. The lesson plan should include headers, such as objectives, the major topics that are covered, the program time frame, required equipment and materials, and the learning activities used to support the training. The plan may be broken down into individual modules or lessons.

I like to develop lesson plans similar to outlines that frame the training and the content. Here is what I include in a typical training or lesson plan:

- Title of the program
- Purpose or training goal statement
- Audience
- Length of the course
- Learning objectives
- Module description or learning outline
- Learning methods and format, and time frame
- Audiovisuals and instructor notes

Lesson plans can also be used for developing a detailed trainer's guide. The training guide or instructor's guide furnishes the trainer with step-by-step directions on how to deliver the program content. Exhibit 4.1 offers a sample lesson plan on conflict management.

Determine Learning Methodologies

After determining the training program's content, the next step is to develop learning methodologies or the methods by which the learning occurs. In today's world of training, most participants want active learning involvement, where they are involved and entertained in the learning environment. The reality is that

Exhibit 4.1 Sample Lesson Plan (Conflict Management)

Program title: Communication Skills
Lesson: Conflict Management
Objectives: (1) Identify what conflict is and is not, as well as sources of conflict.
            (2) Identify individual conflict styles.
            (3) Explain five-step process to resolve conflict.
Materials: Flipchart, video, conflict styles methodology.

Time	Content	Methodology	Resource
00:00–00:10	Define conflict.	Lecture	Participant book (page 1)
	Ask group to identify sources of conflict.	Small-group discussion	
00:20–00:35	Review conflict styles instrument instructions.	Lecture	Conflict style inventory
	Ask participants to complete.	Individual assessment	
	Review each style.	Lecture	Flipchart
00:35–00:50	Present video on managing conflict.	Video	
	Discuss five-step process to resolve conflict, and ask group for examples.	Small-group discussion	

adults learn differently than children do. Adult learning is based on their own experiences. Adults are more self-directed in their learning; therefore, trainers need to show adult trainees the practical benefits of what they are being taught, as well as create an environment that draws on their own experiences.

Learning is promoted best in an informal learning environment where participants have a great deal of control over their learning. Another key with adults is to use a variety of learning activities to help keep the participants motivated and stimulated. Interactive learning helps to ensure that the training makes a lasting impression.

Since adults prefer engaging or involving learning environments, one of the challenges is to design an effective learning experience. There are a wide variety of instructional methods available to create an engaging learning environment.

Types of instruction range from lecture and role playing to assessment and small-group discussion.

In determining the best methods possible, consider the available time, the group, its experience with the topic, and its size. There are a variety of instructional methods, described next.

Role Play or Skills Practice. Role playing or skills practice involves practicing a particular situation or scenario, with each participant taking a specific role. Role plays are similar to doing a play, with each participant assuming a role or part. They usually receive some direction on how to behave in the scenario. For example, in a role play on holding a performance discussion, someone would assume the role of the manager and another participant would be the employee.

Role plays can be done in large or small groups. In a large-group format, the role play is held in front of the other participants, who observe the situation. I prefer using role plays in small groups where the class role-plays simultaneously.

Discussion. Discussions are group forums that focus on specific predetermined questions. They can occur in small groups, where four or five people discuss a particular topic. If small groups are used, there often follows a large-group discussion to synthesize the information. To give an example, "In small groups, please discuss and identify five changes you have observed in health care over the last three to four years." After the small-group discussion, the trainer leads a discussion with the whole group that identifies themes, similarities, and differences.

Games. Games are fun, interactive activities that allow participants to solve problems or use particular skills. I have seen trainers develop games based on popular television shows like "Jeopardy" or "Wheel of Fortune" to help illustrate or review skills that the training covers. In a financial basics program, for example, the trainer used a Jeopardy format to quiz the participants on the terms and concepts of the profit-and-loss statement. There are many books of games for all situations; some are included in the resource listing of Chapter Nine.

Assessment. Assessments are usually done individually and permit the participant insight into his own skill level. As a trainer, assessments are a good way of giving the participants a reason to participate in the training; if you complete an assessment, you can learn where you need to improve your skills. For a listening course, an assessment might be to evaluate listening skills. There are many training resources available that offer assessment tools on a variety of topics.

Case Studies. Case studies are written examples of a specific situation and how the situation is handled. Case studies help the participants learn concepts while applying them to specific situations. In a delegation program for nursing, a case study might list a variety of tasks, and the participants then determine which tasks they would delegate. Case studies can be either purchased or created. If you are planning to write a case study, keep in mind that the case should be relevant and realistic. It needs to be easy to follow and contain specific information on the concepts the case is written about.

Demonstrations. Demonstrations are used to give participants a chance to practice their skill level in a controlled setting. In these cases, the instructor demonstrates a technique and the participant mimics the demonstration, as in demonstrating how to draw blood or take blood pressure.

Lecture. Lectures are trainer-led, content-specific presentations on a particular topic. Typically, a lecture gives an overview and key steps or components of a specific topic, say, steps a manager needs to take to document a performance problem. Lectures work best in small doses and when the trainer uses good presentation skills. Nothing is more boring than a trainer lecturing for an entire program—or worse yet, just reading. Chapter Five is devoted to training delivery. In the meantime, here are a few presentation techniques that I have found useful:

- Do not read your presentation. Use notes if you must, but don't read the information word for word. Put yourself into the presentation by providing your own examples and stories.

- Speak clearly, loudly, and slowly. Practice taking breaths during your talk. Avoid rushing through the material. Vary your pitch and tone. Smile.

- Start with a strong opening, reinforce the concepts throughout, and end with a strong closing that summarizes the learning.

- Use flipcharts or demonstrations to illustrate your main points.

Action Plan or Development Planning. Action planning is often used in training to help participants develop a plan on how to use the particular skill in the workplace. For example, at the end of a training program on recognition and motivation, the participant identifies who she will recognize and motivate and how she will do it. Action plans should force the participant to be as specific as possible and include both actions and time frames. In some cases, they incorporate review of the course content with the manager and trainer. Exhibit 4.2 is a sample of a generic action plan useful in a variety of training programs. Note that the plan incorporates preplanning activities into the action-planning process.

Assignments. Assignments in training are similar to assignments in school. They are tasks relating to the training material that the participant needs to complete as a way to demonstrate learning. For example, participants could write a business plan at the end of a business planning program. In developing assignments, make sure they are relevant and useful to the participant. No one wants to do busy work.

Tests. A test is a means of verifying how well the participant has learned the training subject matter. At the end of a pharmacology course, the participant might determine the correct dosage of medications. Tests can be constructed in a variety of ways; they can be subjective (short answers or essays) or objective (true-false or multiple choice). The subject matter normally dictates the type of test to use. There are a host of books written on test construction; see Chapter Nine for some samples.

Reading and Writing Exercises. Reading and writing exercises normally include reading a particular passage and responding to questions in writing. In an interviewing course, for example, participants are asked to read a passage on the kinds of questions that can and cannot be asked in an interview. They are then asked to rewrite the questions that are worded incorrectly.

Computer-Based Training (CBT). CBT is a great tool for teaching a variety of skills. CBT is a computer-based program that the participant completes at his convenience. They are designed to include content, which the participant reads, and exercises that the participant completes using a computer. At the end of the

Exhibit 4.2 Sample Participant Workshop Planner

Let's prepare for your upcoming training session. If you don't spend time focusing on what you want from this specific training session, you will probably walk away disappointed with the information, techniques, and/or skills being shared.

Part 1 (Employee or Participant)
Planning

This section is to be completed prior to the training session. Please complete this section by (date) _____ .

List those learning objectives from the course information that you think will best serve your training needs. It should be noted that although you are listing two or three objectives, others will appear as you participate in the training.

Objective #1: _____

_____

Objective #2: _____

_____

Part 2 (Employee and Supervisor)
First Discussion

This is an important time to discuss your training plans with your supervisor. It is also the time for the employee and supervisor to discuss the training objectives and identify any particular aspect of the training that the supervisor sees as beneficial to the employee's professional growth.

Part 3 (Employee)
Implementing and Processing the Training

This section is to be completed immediately following the training experience.
What are the most important new skills, techniques, and/or knowledge that you gained by attending the training that will be an asset to you in performing your job duties and responsibilities?

Action Plan

Describe in specific detail the problem and/or situation where improvement is needed.

Describe your plan for addressing the problem or situation and using the training. It is important that you identify who will do what (resources), when it will be completed (date), and how you will know when you have successfully met your goal.

CBT module, the participant completes a test to validate learning. CBT is used for a host of skills (such as sexual harassment training for managers) as well as clinical skills. There are many vendors of JCAHO-approved CBT programs for mandatory competencies.

Self-Paced Learning. Self-paced learning may consist of reviewing a workbook or video and completing exercises. It is useful if there are a few individuals who need training, or if there are prerequisites prior to the training event. For example, in a self-directed learning packet for telephone skills, the participant might watch a videotape and complete a workbook.

On-the-Job Training (OJT). OJT provides training at the participant's worksite. It may include use of a mentor or preceptor to monitor skill development and extend feedback. In addition, the learning might incorporate development assignments to give the learner an opportunity to practice the skills in action; for example, a nursing assistant might have clinical OJT to practice drawing blood.

Learning Teams. Learning teams are cross-functional teams that constitute a forum for dialogue and learning. The team can be set up to discuss books and articles, or to review particular theories or concepts. Several organizations have set up networks of learning teams as a means of supplementing their own management and leadership development plan.

Learning teams can be chartered in a variety of ways. Typically they follow the format of reading groups. Managers and employees need to discuss a particular book or article, and a facilitator provides the format for discussion through questions that assist the employees in making the leap from concepts to the reality of the workplace. Learning teams can also be used to educate employees on new concepts or theories. The key to learning team success is having an excellent facilitator who knows how to select materials that support the organization's mission.

Each of these learning activities can be used in a multitude of program types. They work well in clinical or nonclinical settings. As a trainer, I like to use a variety of activities to make my training engaging and interesting. The key is to experiment and create a fun atmosphere—but be sure all activities are focused on the training objectives.

Design Program Materials

There are a number of considerations when designing program materials. First and foremost, is classroom training the most effective means of teaching the program content? Classroom programs are expensive, and other less-expensive and equally viable methods exist, including job aids and self-learning packets.

Job Aids. Job aids are easily referenced materials that remind a trainee of specific procedures. A job aid may be a card that illustrates how to use a particular piece of equipment, or perhaps a guide that explains how to register a patient. Job aids are very helpful if the participant does not use the skill frequently.

Here are two sample job aids.

In Case of Fire . . .

R   Rescue/Remove patients from danger.

A   Alarm: pull fire alarm and call 12345.

C   Confine the fire; close doors and windows.

E   Extinguish, if possible. Evacuate as necessary.

Steps for Resolving Conflict

1. State the problem.

- Describe the situation specifically.
- State why it concerns you.
- Be positive and patient.

2. Clarify the details.

- Provide specific examples.
- Ask for other points of view.
- Summarize.

3. Search for a solution.

- Explore alternatives to resolve the situation.
- Be flexible.

4. Evaluate and agree.

- Use the other person's ideas.

- Seek agreement.

- Decide who will do what by when.

Self-Learning Packet. We have just reviewed the benefits of self-learning packets as an instructional aid. They are also a wonderful way to impart individual training, since they are inexpensive and work particularly well to respond to individual training needs. A self-paced learning packet should be able to stand on its own. In essence, it is a self-contained training program. The packet should rely on activities such as assessments, reading and writing assignments, questions and answers, and problems and action planning. It requires complete directions and descriptions, since the learner does not have the benefit of an instructor. Exhibit 4.3 is a sample of a self-learning packet for observers.

Whether job aids, self-learning packets, or classroom handouts, all training materials should follow some basic design principles.

Design Principles

In designing training materials, it is important to use these key principles; they add polish to your materials and enhance the trainer's credibility.

Visibility. Materials must be easy to see and read. Readability is increased by using a large font, accented with color, boldface, or italics. Major concepts or key learning should be highlighted with supporting information. Materials should also include plenty of white space. Nothing is worse than materials that are crowded and difficult to read.

Accessibility. All materials should be written using common language. Avoid difficult terms. If there is potential for misunderstanding, clarify the material with simple, active language.

Graphic Flair. Include attention-grabbing devices such as boxes, shading, bullet points, charts, graphs, and graphics. In clinical programs, diagrams are also a useful method for reinforcing the concepts. Cartoons can add punch to even the driest material.

Exhibit 4.3 Sample of a Self-Learning Packet for Observers

DIRECTIONS

Read the book carefully. At the end of the information, there are review questions. Read the questions and select the correct answer. After completing the test, enter completion of the Observer Module into your continuing-education record. Answer sheet must be returned to your manager, to be filed in your record. Please discuss any questions you may have with your manager.

EXCERPTS OF MATERIALS FROM THE PACKET

Objectives

Upon completion of this self-learning module, the learner will be able to:

1. Define *observer*
2. Distinguish between suicide precautions and safety observations
3. Identify at least three key responsibilities of an observer

Responsibility of the Observer

Arrive on time at the designated area, and in proper attire. Introduce yourself to the RN in charge of the patient you are assigned to observe. (Give your name and title.)

Obtain a brief report on patient, including patient's name, whether the patient is on suicide or safety precautions, and the level of activity patient may perform (e.g., bed rest, out of bed to chair, ambulatory).

Guidelines for Suicide Precautions

- *Never* leave patient alone or out of your sight for a moment!

- If patient is ambulatory, you must walk everywhere with him or her; if the patient goes off the unit for tests, you must go along.

- Position yourself between the patient and the door. Never put yourself in a corner where you could be trapped.

- Be aware of your surroundings and what items could be used as a weapon for the patient to harm himself or herself, or you. (Utensils should be plastic; when the patient is finished eating, all utensils should leave the room. Do not put them in the trash where the patient could get them out again. Ask the RN before supplying the patient with pens, pencils, razors, or any other items that could be harmful.)

- Bathroom door must always remain *open!*

Professionalism. Grammatical or spelling errors immediately detract from the credibility of material. Take time to ensure that materials are accurate.

Usefulness. Keep in mind the difference between need-to-know and nice-to-know information. (Many people have books or manuals on their shelves that have never been opened.) Also, include a list of references or resources for the trainee who may wish to pursue a topic further.

Organization. Materials should be organized to support the lesson plan. It is distracting to have a participant shuffling papers to keep up with the trainer. Use page numbers or dividers to help, and begin with a title page. It should include the program title, the trainer's name, and the training program date.

Exhibit 4.4 is a sample of participant materials for a visioning exercise.

Determine Evaluation Methods

The last step in the design process is determining the evaluation methods. Chapter Six explores training evaluation in depth.

CONCLUSION

In this chapter we have reviewed the basics of training design. Specifically, we looked at the process that I use in training design, from creating a purpose statement and objectives to developing the content and methodology and finally designing materials and evaluation methods. We also examined ways to make training creative, interesting, and energetic. In reality, designing a great training program takes a significant amount of energy. It also takes time to create learning objectives, write lesson plans, and determine learning activities. Most great training designs look effortless. Well, looks are deceiving. Training is hard work, but spending the time up front ensures program success. A great design is only half the battle, but the test is to deliver the training in a manner that makes the participant want to learn. In the next chapter, we explore in detail skills for delivering training.

Exhibit 4.4 Sample of Participant Materials (Visioning Exercise)

Visioning Exercise for Transformational Leadership

A well-defined vision is critical to transformational leadership. Use the Nursing Care Delivery Plan, your unit profile, the self-assessment material, and the questions below to define your vision of yourself as a transformational leader.

- What do I want to achieve?
- What does this department look like under my leadership?
- What do I need to do to get there?
- What are my strengths and weaknesses?
- Which of my fellow leaders' skills can I capitalize on?
- What are my grounding values? How do they relate to the mission statement I developed?
- What experiences do I need to make this transformation occur?
- What kind of help do I need and who do I need it from?
- How will I know the department and I are successful?
- What are our measures of success?
- Who do I need feedback from?
- What changes do I need to make?
- What behaviors do I need to role-model?

How to Deliver Training

In the last chapter, we looked at how to design effective training programs. Now we discuss delivering dynamic training. In particular, we focus on how to create a positive learning climate for trainees through using verbal and nonverbal delivery skills, learning styles, popular training aids and audiovisuals, strategies for handling common classroom situations, and do's and don'ts for trainers.

The chapter closes with a discussion of how trainers also use facilitation skills in their work with large and small groups. Specifically, we take a look at the basic facilitation skill of attending and questioning, as well as the familiar concepts that make up excellent facilitation skills.

ON STAGE: A PERSPECTIVE

Joyce, an employee development trainer, is set to deliver a training program on listening skills. After spending the last few weeks on designing the program, she now shifts her attention to preparing for the program. Let's see how she gets ready to deliver the program.

First, as part of the training design, Joyce develops training games and exercises to add interest and emphasize major points.

Second, she reviews the presentation design and creates instructor's notes. She develops a time line and points at which she'll designate breaks. Joyce also works to create effective transitions between topics and sections.

Next, she creates visual aids: flipcharts, overheads, and other visuals. She reviews the video she is planning to use and creates a discussion aid to help review the major points of the video.

Joyce now is ready to practice. She works through the design with a few colleagues to make sure that the timing is correct; that the exercises work; and that there are clear transitions, introductions, and summaries. She memorizes her introductory comments so she can get off to a terrific start.

The day before the program, she sets up the room and organizes the training materials. She uses a checklist to make sure that she has the supplies she needs.

On the big day, Joyce arrives early to do a final review and to greet participants.

She begins by using her prepared introduction. She then shares her expectations for the program with the participants, including the need for participation, time commitments, and learning goals.

As you can see, this example illustrates the importance of careful preparation and rehearsal in delivering a dynamic training program. Joyce's success depends not only on the design but also on what she does to create a positive learning climate. She spends time preparing for the actual training delivery by carefully rehearsing, developing learner-centered activities, and creating interesting visual aids. Additionally, she gets her program off to a great start by arriving early to greet participants and by sharing learning expectations up front.

Now let's discuss other components of successful delivery:

- Verbal and nonverbal presentation skills
- Learning styles
- Training aids
- Handling common classroom problems
- Additional do's and don'ts

Verbal and Nonverbal Presentation Skills

Having a great training design does not guarantee a program's success. The trainer's ability to create a positive learning environment depends on using a variety of delivery methods: verbal and nonverbal presentation skills that set the stage for success.

Voice. One of the best assets of any trainer is his voice. An effective speaking voice should have a number of characteristics:

- Projection. The voice is easily heard throughout the classroom.
- Expressiveness. It uses a variety of intonation and inflection to convey meaning.
- Naturalness. The voice has an affable tone; pacing allows the trainee to listen over a long period of time.

If you are unsure of your voice quality, use a recorder to tape your voice and listen to it. Better yet, ask *others* to listen to your voice and critique it. (The people are few and far between who like listening to their own recorded voice!)

Body Language. Nonverbal skills help to keep participants' attention focused on the learning presentation. Body language, which includes posture and movement, can reinforce the point the trainer is making. Always stand straight and tall to convey confidence in the subject you are teaching. In addition, using movement emphasizes the importance of a particular point or concept. The only reservation about movement is that is should be meaningful. Think about watching a play on stage; when an actor moves, all eyes are on her. She captures our attention. Likewise, trainees watch what the trainer is doing. Meaningless movement can detract from the speaker and the message.

Gestures. Ever watch someone who talks with his hands? After a while, you end up focusing entirely on the hands, and the concepts to be conveyed are totally lost. For gestures to be effective, they have to be intentional—a specific movement that reinforces a specific point or concept. The general rule is that gestures above the shoulders are normally thought to exhibit inspiration and excitement, while gestures below the waist are viewed negatively.

Facial Expressions. Facial expressions are an easy way to reinforce your message. Simply smile! Trainees want to be around people who are positive about the concepts they are teaching. For facial expressions to be successful, they should be congruent with the intended message. If you are unsure of what your expressions are conveying, ask friends for feedback, or rehearse some of your presentation in front of a mirror.

Eye Contact. Establishing eye contact with participants is an easy way to engage them in the learning environment. Focusing a few seconds on particular trainees helps to build relationships and at the same time continue putting them at ease. Think of "visiting with each participant," that is, holding eye contact for the amount of time it takes to complete a thought.

As a trainer, I have found that by paying attention to these verbal and nonverbal presentation skills I add polish to my training programs. To practice these skills, I suggest two great methods. First, a class on presentation skills offers individual feedback. Typically, the class includes taping your presentation, which gives you immediate feedback on your skills. Second, join a local Toastmasters club. This is an international organization meant to give members a chance to practice their presentation skills. It allows guidance on how to speak effectively in public and offers peer support as you refine your skills.

Learning Styles

In addition to verbal and nonverbal delivery skills, another critical element in successful training is the ability to understand a variety of learning styles. Individuals learn differently. Some people learn by picturing what is going on; others learn most effectively from hands-on practice, and still others learn best from lecture or hearing. *Learning style* refers to how learners respond to a variety of learning experiences. The three key three learning styles are visual, auditory, and tactile.

Visual Learning. Visual learners take information in by seeing pictures of it, watching demonstrations, and viewing films. They must see it to understand it. Therefore, your classes should include one or more visual aids: reading information, overheads, flipcharts, or videos. I like using videos; they are entertaining and are an excellent way to illustrate key points. Videos exist on most topics, from safety to diversity, from aseptic technique to how to conduct a meeting.

Many production companies send a preview video to determine if it works with the content. When previewing a video, it is important to assess the length, the topics covered, the method of discussing the topics, and how up-to-date it is (does the wardrobe look dated? is it diverse in terms of gender and race?). Videos specific to health care and health care settings are available. This is helpful, since most health care employees see the industry as unique. American Media Incorporated is a wonderful resource for videos specific to health care. Contact information is in Chapter Nine, in the listing of videos.

Auditory Learning. Other trainees might need to hear the concepts to assimilate them. They prefer to learn by listening; they like to take information in from lectures and audiotapes. To ensure auditory learning, you can rely on audiotapes or group discussion to support content development, along with well-presented lecture material.

Tactile Learning. For still other learners, nothing takes the place of actually doing or practicing the concepts. Tactile learners like hands-on activities; they enjoy asking questions and respond well to activities such as games and simulation that allow them to actively engage in the skill being taught.

Let's see how a trainer uses all three styles in delivering a training program. Abbie recently developed a training program on proofreading skills. She used several delivery methods to meet various learners' needs.

First, she created a manual and video (visual) to illustrate the key components of a proofreading system. Next, she designed interactive proofreading exercises for participants to practice their new skills (tactile), and lastly she recorded a short audiotape of key points for participants to use as reinforcement (auditory). If you want to learn more about learning styles, I recommend checking out some of the resources offered by ASTD (the American Society for Training and Development) or Jossey-Bass Pfeiffer; see Chapter Nine for specific information.

TRAINING AIDS

After determining the learning style, you can then focus attention on a few key training aids that are used to help teach the content of your training program. Training aids serve a variety of purposes. They underscore key points, increase interest in the content by making it visually appealing, and improve retention of the information by engaging a variety of learning styles. We begin our discussion with a brief introduction to visual aids in general and then concentrate on flipcharts, overhead transparencies, and videotapes.

Visual Aids

Most trainers use visual aids at some point in delivery. They are designed to support the concepts of training by reinforcing important concepts and highlighting the key points. Visuals can also help the trainer by improving the learner's retention of the important information.

Add punch and pizzazz to any visual by considering eight pointers:

1. Keep visuals simple. They work best when focused on one idea or concept. Use the KISS principle (Keep It Simple, Sweetheart) when planning and designing your visual aids.

2. Use color on your flipcharts, overheads, or computer-generated slides. Two or three colors can be used to highlight, organize, and capture attention. Also, no more than six lines of content, please! Keep lots of white space on your visual.

3. Use bullets or key words to capture ideas, as opposed to whole sentences. Think big and bold.

4. Use pictures, graphics, and symbols to represent the important concepts on your visuals.

5. The world's worst visual aid is a white typewritten page.

6. Consider bringing along actual objects to help emphasize the key points.

7. Use a variety of visual aids to add interest to your presentation.

8. Analyze the visual with this straightforward test: Is it clear, visible, and simple?

Flipcharts. As a trainer, I think our slogan should be "Have flipchart, will travel." No tool is more synonymous with training than the simple flipchart. Whether used to capture participants' thoughts and ideas or to lay out lessons, the flipchart works best in small groups. The size of the chart and readability make it unwieldy in a large-group setting.

Flipcharts are typically used in two ways: to prepare information, or to capture information during the training session. In either case, you should make your flipcharts as readable and interesting as possible.

Some flipchart pointers:

- Print letters at least two inches high.

- Don't write more than six lines with six words in each line on each page.

- Highlight key points using graphics, boxes, and shapes.

- Use the top three-quarters of the chart. Leave the bottom empty because participants sitting in the back of the room normally can't see the bottom of the chart.

- Use color to add visual interest. Limit colors to no more than three per chart. Also consider using darker colors; they are easier to read. (I recommend Mr. Sketch water-based markers; they don't bleed through the chart paper.)

- Use the "turn-touch-talk" technique. When you show the visual, *turn* to it with your body at a 45-degree angle to the group, *touch* or point to the visual as you look at it, and then look back at the audience and *talk* to them. Similarly, avoid writing on the flipchart with your back to the audience. Consider instead keeping your body at the recommended 45-degree angle, and maintain some eye contact with the group.

Overhead Transparencies. Along with flipcharts, overhead transparencies are quite commonly used as visual aids. This is because they are especially useful with medium-sized groups. As a trainer, I find transparencies easy to use. They are presentation triggers or "cue cards" that I can refer to. They allow me to talk to the audience without a lot of stirring through notes and guides. The key to using transparencies is to spend time planning their design. Here are some guidelines to consider in designing outstanding overheads:

- Use as few words as possible to convey an idea.

- Keep ideas to six words per line, six lines per transparency.

- Cover only one major idea in each transparency.

- Illustrate ideas with pictures, graphics, bullets, and colors.

- Keep all overheads consistent in look: all "landscape" in orientation (as opposed to the vertical portrait alternative), similar fonts, and consistent colors.

- Turn the projector off between overheads, unless you are showing them in rapid succession.

- Use a pointer or pencil to focus trainee attention on a particular area.

- Consider uncovering the overhead one point at a time by using a piece of paper to mask the overhead and revealing each point when needed. Again, this helps focus the trainee's attention.

- Use the familiar stiff-paper frames to give a finished look to the overheads. You can also make notes to yourself on the frame regarding what to say or point out in addition to what is on the transparency.

Computer-generated overhead transparencies are becoming the standard format for most presentations. Software such as Microsoft PowerPoint offers an easy way to create polished transparencies. These systems are also a framework to help you design overheads consistently. They can be used in conjunction with In-Focus machines (which project the computer-generated presentation on a large screen), thus eliminating the need for overhead projectors.

Videotapes. One easy way to create interest and illustrate key points or concepts is to use videotapes. The reality is that today's workers are of the TV generation; they respond to training aids that stimulate their senses and are visually interesting. Videotapes fit the bill.

Most trainers use commercial videotapes for training classes. Videos can support the training topic, as with one that illustrates the change process for a change management class. Videos can also form the basis of the training, for example, a videotape-based training program in which the trainer provides the facilitation and the video presents the instruction.

In selecting a commercial video, I usually look for certain attributes:

- A high-quality product. Is the videotape current? Is the content sophisticated enough? Is the product professional looking—that is, are the picture and sound of good production quality?

- Diversity. Does the video present a variety of races, cultures, ages, and concepts?

- Appropriateness. Do the concepts match the intended purpose of the training program? Do they reinforce your training program?

- A health care focus, whenever possible. Several video production companies now have training videos specific to health care. See Chapter Nine for suggestions.

If you are using videos, it is important to keep a couple of further things in mind.

Preparation. First, you need to review the tape in advance of the program to make sure that you are comfortable with it. Don't forget to rewind the videotape to make sure it is ready to go for the start of the training program. If you are going to use only portions or segments of the videotape, use the counter to make sure that you can fast forward to the right section, and on the day of the program make sure that the VCR's counter is set correctly. (And remember that your reliance on the counter can also be sabotaged if another VCR is substituted at the last minute!) Another tip is to set up the videotape prior to the training program. Fast forward through all the introductory messages so the tape begins playing where you want it to.

Introduce the videotape. I always provide a short introduction to the video: why I chose this particular tape, what the tape covers, and any instructions for the participants ("You will need to take notes on the key points covered in the video").

After the videotape. Summarize the key points and ideas that were covered in the tape, or hold a discussion with the participants on the key ideas and then transition to the next topic.

In summary, videotapes are an easy way to add visual appeal to your next training program. They are easy to use and can create fun and excitement by reinforcing a learning concept. There are myriad training video resources to help you select a video that works for your next program; see Chapter Nine for specific resources.

In addition to commercial videos, you might also look at options from television and movies. For example, *Twelve Angry Men* is a classic film that illustrates a variety of conflict styles. *The Wizard of Oz* beautifully portrays the power of teamwork. Television clips from talk shows and sitcoms can often be used to illustrate various communication skills. If you do use excerpts from any TV shows, though, make sure you check out copyright regulations.

Other Creative Training Aids. Learning can be fun through using creative visual aids. Props, games, rewards, prizes, and themes can make the learning delightful for you the trainer, and the participant.

A colleague once taught me an important lesson: "Adults are kids in big bodies." Most adults want to be entertained and stimulated. By incorporating even a small number of creative aids, you can increase your own effectiveness and that of the training.

In thinking about creative ideas, be sure to avoid doing things that might be considered hokey, or games that make adults feel foolish. Instead, consider using some of these more appropriate devices.

Props. Especially useful in a clinical training setting, props can illustrate vital concepts for demonstration and practice, as with a prosthetic arm for practice in inserting IVS. Props can also be used to reinforce topics or ideas; a colleague uses a variety of props such as Lifesavers, pillows, and plants to illustrate a variety of recognition concepts. For example, to thank an employee who helps out, my colleague uses Lifesaver candy to illustrate how to recognize an employee who is a real life saver.

Games. Any game can be adapted for use in a training program, as with using Jeopardy-style games to test knowledge. The key is to think about the purpose of your program, and the best way and format to involve participants in a fun and easy-to-use game that increases their knowledge and understanding. One caution with games is that you need to know your audience. I am not sure, for example, that I would want to use a game with a certain group of physicians I can think of!

There are plenty of readily available games, and like videotapes, there are numerous resources that sell games for a variety of purposes. One of the most popular is Edward Scannell's *Games Trainers Play* and *More Games Trainers Play,* both available through ASTD.

Rewards and prizes. Consider giveaways and prizes as rewards for training. Prizes can be used to reward participants who ask questions, or who come back from lunch or break on time. Prizes can be as simple as candy or more substantial, depending on the number and budget. At a recent training program, we gave each participant a copy of *Flawless Consulting* by Peter Block, which related well to the subject matter of the course (staff consulting skills).

Themes. A theme serves to reinforce the training program by capturing its concepts. It can be illustrated through decorations, materials, prizes, and games. A colleague used the theme of the *Wizard of Oz* as a metaphor for change and teamwork. She created props, including a yellow brick road for the floor, ruby red boxes for each table that held candy, and posters with characters encountered in various modules. Talk about creativity!

HANDLING COMMON CLASSROOM PROBLEMS

Although training aids often add to the effectiveness of a program, it remains a crucial skill for the trainer to be able to handle classroom problem situations effectively. Every trainer, new or experienced, runs into occasional problem situations. They often involve participants whose behavior prevents or inhibits learning. Here is an example of such a situation and how the trainer handled it.

Ben, an employee development trainer, was asked to conduct customer-service training for an entire organizational unit. During the session, three trainees voiced concerns about the program and the topic, saying things on the order of "We don't need this. This is a waste of time." Nor did these participants participate in the program. Ben tried to address their concerns by reviewing the objectives and benefits of the program.

During a break, he also asked them probing questions to find out what, if any, training needs they felt they needed. He also invited their participation, saying, "Although you may not want to be here, I feel certain the group would benefit from your participation."

Then, after the program, he went back to the leaders of the organizational group and asked them to make opening remarks for future sessions that would illustrate their expectations for the program.

His choices demonstrate a number of ways to handle classroom behavior. He first responded by clarifying the connection between the program content and the participants' jobs. He then used questioning skills to better understand their concerns. He tried to encourage their participation by showing them respect.

Finally, he developed a plan to have senior management clarify both the purpose of the training program and their expectations of participants.

Over the course of my career, I have also dealt with this type of resistance. To overcome it, I usually work with managers to make sure they explain up front the reason participants are attending the session, and then at the beginning of the session I always review the objectives and benefits of the session.

Another problem is handling personal attacks. Sometimes learners challenge you as a trainer by questioning your authority or credibility. In handling these attacks, it is important to remain calm and controlled, and to avoid defensiveness. Let's say you are a clinical nurse and are giving your first course on communication with patients. A participant challenges you, "What do you know about communications?" Remaining calm, you reply, "I may not know everything about communications, but I definitely know a lot about patients, and I have a firm handle on my ideas and experiences in communications, especially in a health care setting." The key is to stop the behavior and keep the participant engaged by continuing to show the participant respect.

Side conversation is another common classroom problem. Small groups may talk while you are presenting information. Whether the individuals are discussing relevant topics or not, side conversations are distracting. To handle this situation, consider:

1. Calling on one of the individuals and asking him to respond to a question

2. Asking them to respond to the last point that you or another participant made

3. Standing near the group to help refocus their attention

4. Stopping and asking them directly if there is something they would like to add to the discussion

DO'S AND DON'TS FOR TRAINERS

Delivering training takes skills and practice. Whether you are a new or experienced trainer, it is important to keep in mind some simple do's and don'ts of excellent delivery skills. Let's review some of the key points in the chapter by way of a list of valuable do's and don'ts for delivering a dynamic training program.

Do's

Here are examples of things to do to deliver great programs.

Prepare in Advance. The most important thing trainers can do is prepare. This means everything from content to delivery methods and evaluation. Everything should be reviewed and rehearsed to make sure the pieces fit together. For me, preparation also means developing transitions or ways to move from one topic to another, and contingency planning (what I will do if I run short on time? if I run out of materials?). I always develop alternatives for activities and determine in advance what I can cut out if I need to.

Develop a Strong Introduction. I always try to develop a strong introduction to my training programs. I want to make a great first impression, so I take time to really think about an interesting way to begin. As part of the introduction, I review the objectives of the program, as well as benefits. Additionally, I clarify the participants' expectations regarding participation.

Make Your Session Interactive. Adults learn through experience, that is, by having the opportunity to practice the content. As a trainer, I try to make my training sessions engaging by offering choices about the activities, using group exercises, and asking for feedback and questions.

Develop a Professional Training Demeanor. As a trainer, I try to develop the most professional training demeanor possible. For me, this means:

- Dressing professionally. Sloppy attire affects the participants' perception of you and the materials.
- Arriving early for the session. I like to arrive at least thirty to forty-five minutes ahead of time to prepare the room and my training materials. In addition, by arriving early, I am able to introduce myself to the participants and learn about their interests before the actual class begins.

Put Yourself at Ease. It is natural to feel nervous about training. After fifteen years, I still have to cope with nerves sometimes. To put myself at ease, I practice these techniques:

- I rehearse the training program to make sure that I feel comfortable.
- I memorize my opening to ensure a great start.
- I prepare training aids and review materials well in advance.

- I try to get as much rest as possible the night before the training.
- I wear professional yet comfortable clothing and shoes to enhance my comfort level.

Don'ts

Remember these don'ts, which create problems for many trainers.

Not Following the Time Guidelines. It is important to follow the agenda that allows you to complete the workshop in a timely manner. As a trainer, you should pay special attention to exercise and break times, and constantly readjust the training agenda to meet the program's needs.

Relying on Just One Delivery Method. Nothing is more boring than relying on one method to deliver training. Effective trainers vary their delivery methods to ensure interest and retention of the information.

Not Keeping the Program Fresh. No matter how often you teach a particular program, it is important to remember that for the participant in attendance, it's the first time. Effective trainers keep their programs fresh by constantly reviewing the content and changing exercises and activities.

FACILITATION SKILLS

Earlier in the chapter we discussed training delivery skills. Facilitation skills, by contrast, help the trainer working with the learners to bridge the gap between the training content and the learners' applications to their work world. There are major differences between training and facilitation. First, training focuses on a structured learning environment where the trainer leads and is the catalyst for learning. The facilitator, on the other hand, manages the process and not the content. The participants are catalysts for learning, and the facilitator's job is to engage the learners in the learning process. Here is an example to illustrate these differences.

Ann is a trainer who has been asked to conduct a session on team effectiveness. She designs a structured learning process and lectures to the participants on steps for team effectiveness. The purpose of this class is basically to teach a concept.

Susan, on the other hand, has been asked to facilitate a session on team effectiveness. She leads a discussion with the participants on what their ideal team would look like. She asks them to list drivers and barriers to their team effectiveness, and then she works with the group to develop an action plan of steps needed to achieve their ideal group.

Although both ways create a learning environment, Ann is more of the leader or teacher of content, while Susan serves more as a coach. Facilitation involves two essential skills: attending skills and questioning skills.

Attending Skills

Attending skills are those necessary to show the participants you are paying attention. Attending allows you to encourage participation and to develop rapport with the participants. You are showing them that you value them and are interested in them as learners and people. Typically, attending skills are either verbal or nonverbal.

Verbal skills are the things you say that can encourage participation. To show praise or encourage participants, you might consider saying "Tell me more" or "Excellent point." To clarify or build on ideas, try "That's a good suggestion to add to that point" or "As Michelle mentioned. . . ." To reinforce feelings, "You seem upset about this" or "I can tell this must be difficult for you" can be helpful.

Nonverbal skills relate to the facial expressions that demonstrate support. Try *nodding* to show understanding; *eye contact,* looking briefly at each participant to engage him or her in the learning; and *smiling,* which helps to put participants at ease.

Now, you may be asking yourself, *"Aren't these attending skills also used in a typical training class?"* The answer is yes. The best trainers and facilitators use these attending skills (and the questioning and listening skills described next) in the classroom *and* in facilitated processes such as the team-building effort discussed earlier.

Questioning Skills

Another important facilitation skill is questioning, to invite learner participation and involvement. It can be used to give you feedback on what learning has occurred for participants. Questioning skills incorporate two key components: asking questions, and handling and responding to questions.

Basically there are two types of questions that facilitators can ask: open-ended and closed. Open-ended questions cannot be answered with a yes or no answer. Framed by *what, when, where,* or *how,* these questions are very useful in stimulating thinking and encouraging participation. A simple example of an open-ended question is, "What are some of the times when you were not able to properly insert an IV into the patient's arm?"

Closed-ended questions are those that can be answered yes or no or with a one-word answer. These questions are useful when specific answers are needed, and when you want to close a discussion. "Do you know the procedures to give a patient a bath in bed?" is an example of a closed-ended question.

After determining the type of question to ask, trainers need to consider how to phrase it. Phrasing questions is important so that the participant can focus on the topic or information that you want. In phrasing questions, make sure that you ask clear questions covering a single topic or issue. Consider challenging questions that require the participant to illustrate his learning, and avoid asking trick questions or questions that are ambiguous.

In addition to asking questions, trainers need to know how to handle responses to questions. If the answer is correct, give the participant positive reinforcement such as "Thank you" or "Good point." If the answer is incorrect, you might thank the participant for the effort and then redirect the question: "That's a good try. Does anyone have any other thoughts?"

In responding to questions, keep a couple of points in mind. If the participant asks you a question, you can try to answer it yourself, or ask the class for their ideas, or defer it until later. If you are not able to answer the question, you can tell the participant that you simply don't know the answer. Your willingness to tell the truth helps to build rapport and establish trust. Sometimes I say, "I'm not sure, but I'll find out and let you know." Then I write the question down and ask the participant for her phone extension or e-mail address, thus demonstrating that I will get back to her.

While using attending and questioning skills, trainers should also practice listening skills. The ability to listen well and to demonstrate listening is critical for any professional today. To increase your effective listening skills, listen to the participant to grasp both the content and the meaning of the message (the latter is what I call the subtext of a message, the feelings and real intention of the sender). Also, be aware of distractions that keep you from listening fully. These include environmental matters such as clocks, windows, and the other participants, or internal distractions such as thinking about what you are presenting next.

Fully listening involves listening to understand what the participant is saying (the words or content) and meaning (feeling associated with the content). For example, in a recent program a participant was frustrated about the unwillingness of his supervisor to handle a particular issue. What the participant said is, "Nothing works, and my supervisor doesn't help." After probing, I was able to understand the complete context of his situation and his feelings. I was able to reply, "It sounds like a complex situation, and you sound frustrated about your supervisor not being able to deal with the problem." Paraphrasing what has been said demonstrates understanding and helps build rapport with the learner. Participants who feel listened to are able to trust more, which leads to learning.

CONCLUSION

Delivering training programs is critical to training success. Delivery requires preparation. In this chapter we have looked at how to prepare to deliver dynamic training programs. In particular, we focused on how to create a positive learning climate for trainees through using verbal and nonverbal delivery skills, learning styles, popular training aids, strategies for handling common classroom situations, and do's and don'ts for trainers. We ended our discussion on delivery by examining facilitation skills—in particular, attending and questioning skills. Now let's move on to evaluation of training programs, the last section of our training basics overview.

How to Evaluate Training and Institute Follow-up

In the last chapter, we looked at the presentation or delivery skills needed to make training a success. But how does a trainer know if the program worked? How well did the training achieve its objectives? In this chapter, we explore the concept of evaluation, or measuring the program's success. Specifically, we review four levels of evaluation: reaction, learning, behavior, and results. We identify the elements of a successful evaluation plan, as well as the roles of the trainer, manager, and participant in ensuring program success.

EVALUATION: THE BENEFITS

The program is over, so why spend time evaluating training? First, evaluation is an essential part of the training process. It gives the trainer a wealth of information on what worked and did not work in the training design, as well as on the value of the learning experience. Let's look at some of the benefits for engaging in an evaluation process:

- Evaluation is a method to measure the return on investment for training.

- Evaluation ensures that the training program is linked to its primary objectives.

- Evaluation determines how well the trainees understand and practice the concepts and skills taught.

- Evaluation reinforces key learning points and concepts.

- Evaluation provides suggestions for further program development by identifying what works well and what needs to be changed.

Consider evaluation from a trainer's perspective. Kim, a management development trainer, has recently completed designing a program on meeting effectiveness. As part of the training design, she develops her plan for evaluation. In addition to the evaluation she will use at the end of the program, she also decides to test the participants' learning by developing a skills test to ensure that they have achieved the learning objectives. Kim also plans to make sure that the participants are able to conduct an effective meeting by observing their conduct at a meeting in their workplace.

As you see in this example, planning for evaluation is done as part of the training design. Evaluations can be conducted throughout the training and afterwards. Kim also used a variety of evaluation methods as part of the evaluation plan.

The methods are part of the classic four-level evaluation model, derived from the work of Donald Kirkpatrick, the guru of evaluation. The four levels are reaction, learning, behavior, and results. Each level measures certain elements of a program and can be used in tandem with other levels of the model or separately. In many cases, you do not need to apply all levels of evaluation. Most organizations use at least two or three of the four levels.

LEVEL ONE OF EVALUATION: REACTION

Level-one evaluation is called reaction, or, to industry insiders, the "smile sheet." Reaction evaluation is used to determine how well the trainee likes the program. Reaction evaluations measure attendee satisfaction with the content and design, the instructional methods, the trainer's presentation style, and facilities. I always use these evaluations as part of a quick check on a participant's satisfaction with the program.

Reaction evaluations are very easy to construct and use, but they are not the end-all measurement of a program's effectiveness. Typically, reaction evaluation is subjective. In measuring participant satisfaction, the focus is not on measuring learning, but instead on measuring a participant's personal feelings about the class. Here are some guidelines to consider in developing reaction evaluations:

- Be clear about what you want to know. Make a list of the areas you want to query. These might include content, program design, pace, instructional methods, audio and visual elements, trainer's presentation skills, and facilities.

- Keep your form or questionnaire user-friendly. Is it well designed? Does it have space for comments? Does it take little time for the participant to complete?

- Develop a rating scale for the direction of measurement, from negative to positive (1 to 10) or intensity of feeling (poor to excellent). Use an even number of steps on the rating scale, to keep the participant from rating everything exactly in the middle of the scale.

- Use a variety of questions. Include a rating section, as well as a section with open-ended questions.

- Allow participants to respond anonymously. This allows more truthfulness.

- To encourage participants to complete the evaluation, review the form during the opening of the program. This allows them to evaluate the training throughout the program instead of waiting until the end.

Reaction evaluations can be customized for each individual learning event. I like to develop a template that allows me to customize each section with specifics of the program I am training. Exhibit 6.1 is one such evaluation template.

As you can see in the sample, this evaluation is simple and easy to use. It provides a quick reading of all the key components of the program: content, facilities, and presenters.

After the program is complete, I recommend summarizing the evaluations. Assign points to each rating and develop an average. In addition, identify common themes or issues. All of the information generated should be used to continuously improve the training program.

Exhibit 6.1 Template for Program Evaluation

(To be completed by program participant)

Program title: Corporate Compliance Training _____ Date: _____

Facilitator name: _____

Please evaluate the following questions, using this rating scale:

5 = Excellent   4 = Very good   3 = Satisfactory

2 = Fair   1 = Poor   n/a = Not applicable

Program Evaluation	(Completely agree)				(Completely disagree)	
1. The program achieved the stated goals.	5	4	3	2	1	n/a
2. The information presented will be useful in my job.	5	4	3	2	1	n/a
3. The program met my personal objectives.	5	4	3	2	1	n/a
4. The physical environment was conducive to learning.	5	4	3	2	1	n/a
5. The teaching methods used were effective.	5	4	3	2	1	n/a
6. The presentation was well organized.	5	4	3	2	1	n/a
7. Time allowed for discussion was adequate.	5	4	3	2	1	n/a
8. Audiovisuals and handouts enhanced the presentation.	5	4	3	2	1	n/a
How well were the following objectives met?						
1. Recognize the organization's commitment to good compliance practices at all levels.	5	4	3	2	1	n/a
2. Describe the structure and operation of the corporate compliance program.	5	4	3	2	1	n/a
3. Explain the resolution process.	5	4	3	2	1	n/a
4. Identify the hotline operation.	5	4	3	2	1	n/a

Comments or suggestions:

_____

_____

LEVEL TWO: LEARNING

Level two, or learning, evaluation has direct relevance to the health care trainer, who must ensure that a participant has learned the training content, especially in clinical skills programs. The reality is that administrators, managers, and—most important—patients need to feel confident that their caregivers are competent in basic clinical skills.

Learning evaluations can take many forms. They can be tied to activities within the training program, or test the participant's knowledge level. Learning evaluations are more difficult to design and administer than reaction evaluations, but they are very helpful in testing how much participants have retained. Here are some guidelines to consider in developing learning evaluations:

- Tests should be designed to reflect the program objectives.

- Determine the best method to assess knowledge or skills. To measure knowledge, use a paper-and-pencil test. Use a performance test to measure skills.

- In developing paper-and-pencil tests, use objective forms of questioning, such as multiple choice or true-false. Make sure there is only one correct answer for each question. Write questions that are easy to understand, and vary the level of difficulty. Ensure that questions cover all aspects of the training. Write simple and complete directions on how to complete the test.

Sample Patient Care Test Questions

1. True or false: in late adulthood (sixty and older) one can see gradual changes in skin, memory, and mobility.

2. True or false: the main functions of the heart are to pump blood to the lungs to pick up oxygen and get rid of carbon dioxide, and also to pump oxygen to the body and organs.

3. True or false: one can prevent decubitus ulcer by turning patients every two hours; this will prevent cut-off blood circulation.

4. The first step in changing a dressing is to:
   - Put on gloves
   - Gather equipment
   - Wash hands
   - None of the above

For a skill test, ensure that it covers the training and the skills required. Give the participant simple instructions ("I would like you to demonstrate how you draw blood"). Create a standard for each item you are evaluating. This helps you quantify the results.

Learning evaluations can help health care trainers continuously appraise their training programs and determine competence in key clinical areas. In addition, learning evaluations work well in soft skills training. For example, in a team effectiveness program a trainer might consider using a learning evaluation to test participant knowledge of the various stages of team development. Another method for learning evaluation is observation. The trainer can watch or observe the participants role-play, and observe other activities as a means of ensuring that they have learned.

Let's look at a learning evaluation in action.

Beth is conducting a training program on interviewing skills. The objectives are to ensure that managers can effectively conduct a selection interview. In addition, she wants to ensure that the trainees understand what types of questions should and should not be asked. As part of the design, she develops two learning evaluation tools to measure the participants' learning.

First, she devises a simulation that allows her to observe the trainees in action, to determine if they can effectively conduct a selection interview. In addition, she develops a short true-or-false test about legal and illegal types of selection questions.

As you can see, learning evaluations are critical to ensuring participants are able to meet the desired performance. In Beth's case, the two learning evaluations are great opportunities for the participant to practice and for Beth to assess learning.

LEVEL THREE: BEHAVIOR

For most trainers, the evaluation process stops at level two. Yet both reaction and learning evaluations fail to measure whether the training has changed the participant's behavior. Measuring changes in behavior is the focus of evaluation level three.

Level-three, or behavior, evaluation centers on transferring the learning from the classroom to the workplace. For example, in a delegation program, the participants learn the process of delegation. The key to the success of the program is to see if the participant can use the process in delegating assignments in the work environment. This ability is called training transfer. Has the participant transferred the training from the classroom to the workplace? Level-three evaluation is an effective tool in determining the degree of training transfer.

A typical level-three evaluation includes observing the trainee in the workplace and looking for skills taught in the training program. Or it might include interviews of or surveys for the participant and the participant's manager. If using interviews or surveys, include both pretraining and posttraining evaluations. Doing so measures the participant's ability before and after the training.

Another way to assess on-the-job impact of the training is through a focus group or a participant postassessment. Both of these methods require a pretraining and posttraining assessment. Use questions such as, "What is your skill level prior to the training (in percentage)?" and "What is your skill level after completing the course?" In developing a behavior evaluation, consider this pair of guidelines:

- Design the evaluation to include pre- and postassessment.
- Consider designing a long-term evaluation strategy. It is important to assess behavior change in time intervals, such as three and six months.

The manager of a participant in a Fundamentals of Management training program was asked to evaluate the training program participant before the training and three months afterwards. The manager was then asked to complete the questionnaire. Exhibit 6.2 is an excerpt.

LEVEL FOUR: RESULTS

The last and most difficult evaluation is the level-four, or results, evaluation. This is used to determine the actual business results achieved as a product of the training program. Most organizations do not use this type of evaluation. However, as health care organizations increase their investment in training, it is important to have proof of organizational benefits.

Results are often framed in terms of organizational improvement, such as productivity, quality, and quantity. Results evaluations may also measure absenteeism, safety, cost, and turnover. Such evaluations involve analyzing data prior to training and afterwards. For example, prior to conducting a training program on interviewing skills, the trainer assesses the turnover rate in the participant's department. After the program, the trainer then reassesses the turnover rate.

In doing a results evaluation, take into consideration other factors, such as changes in technology or process. Such variables may affect organizational

Exhibit 6.2 Sample Questionnaire for Posttraining Behavior Evaluation

Rating scale:
1 = Strongly disagree   2 = Disagree   3 = Neutral   4 = Agree   5 = Strongly agree

The participant uses individual and group recognition strategies.	1	2	3	4	5
The participant consistently handles employee performance problems in a manner that maintains the employee's self-esteem.	1	2	3	4	5
The participant plans and organizes the daily work of the department to ensure effective delivery of services to patients and customers.	1	2	3	4	5
The participant conducts monthly staff meetings to ensure effective two-way communication methods.	1	2	3	4	5

performance but have no relationship to a completed training program. Suppose an organization invests in a management development program. The next year, the organization's employee satisfaction score soars. It may seem that the results are due to the training program, but one must consider various other changes the organization might have made to improve employee satisfaction.

In constructing a results evaluation, here are two guidelines to consider:

1. Establish baseline data, and focus efforts on a few key result areas rather than all aspects of the training.

2. Frame results in terms of such organizational improvements as productivity, quality, quantity, absenteeism, safety, cost, and turnover.

Here are some sample measures that I have used in my work:

Training Program	Measures
Behavioral interviewing program	Turnover rate of staff
	Transfer rates in and out of departments
Delivering excellent customer service	Patient satisfaction data
Phlebotomy training	Number of complaints
	Number of positive compliments
	Number of successful blood draws
	Number of incorrect blood specimens

Although we touched on the concept of transfer of learning as part of level-three evaluation, transferring learning is of critical importance to trainers. (Such transfers keep us employed!) Here is an example of what I mean. Let's suppose that two trainers are developing programs on customer service. The first develops an excellent program, but he lacks time to create methods to make sure that the skills are practiced in the workplace. The other trainer also develops an excellent program and then spends time ensuring that the skills are used in the workplace; she works with the participants' managers to make sure they know what is being taught so the managers can reinforce the learning.

It is easy to see which trainer and program is the winner. Learning and skills transfer come with a variety of methods; here are a few that are particularly helpful.

FOLLOW-UP SESSIONS

Follow-up sessions often help to reinforce transfer of skills. In follow-up sessions, the participants return after one, two, or three months to discuss what skills they have applied and what has worked and not worked. I love to do follow-up sessions; they allow me to see firsthand if learning has occurred. I also like to hear from the participants what has worked and what has not. I limit follow-up sessions to key programs, since this can be expensive to do and takes time and commitment from the participants and their managers.

The majority of the responsibility in applying training to the job lies with the trainee, but the trainer and the trainee's manager can also assist in maximizing the results of training. Let's take a look at how each role contributes to transfer of learning.

The Participant or Trainee

The participant needs to make a commitment to practice skills. One way participants can commit is by actively participating in the training and creating a plan of action for using the skills in the workplace. Another commitment method is for the participant to meet with her manager to discuss the skills and develop a joint plan of how to use them in the workplace; in a career planning workshop, for instance, I usually require that the participants hold a developmental discussion with their manager.

The Trainee's Manager

The manager also plays a crucial role in creating a bridge from the training program to the workplace. Managers need to identify and eliminate any barriers keeping the trainee from successfully performing the newly acquired skills. They also need to employ positive reinforcement when the trainee practices the new skills.

The Trainer

The trainer can use a couple of simple but powerful techniques to promote training transfer.

The Action Plan

Developed during the training, the action plan is an effective means of clearly defining real-world applications of the skills taught in the classroom. After the training is completed, promote trainee adherence to the action plan created in class. This ensures direct transfer of classroom information to the workplace. Exhibit 6.3 is an example of how to do this.

THE PERSONAL LEARNING CONTRACT

A personal learning contract is a commitment the trainee makes to practice the new skills taught in training. A learning contract might involve continuous follow-up and feedback on the part of the instructor. For example, a trainee may keep a learning log of key actions that were taken during the week, any new learning, and the focus for next week. The trainer should regularly review this log; it is also useful in evaluating the effectiveness of the training program. Exhibit 6.4 is a sample learning contract (or learning log).

CONCLUSION

Evaluation is the trainer's method of ensuring the program meets the needs of the organization. Each level or method is important in the overall design of the evaluation strategy. In this chapter, we have looked at the four levels of evaluation: reaction, learning, behavior, and results. We also explored the variety of methods

Exhibit 6.3 Sample Action Plan Format

Training program: _____

Actions You Will Take as a Result of Attending the Training Program	When Will You Do This?	How Will You Measure Effectiveness?	What Help Do You Need?
Develop an agenda for my next meeting.	3/18	Compare with sample agenda format.	Meet with assistant to review agenda plan.
Review meeting planner format and use to plan the next meeting.	3/18	Use meeting planner after meeting to make sure steps were followed.	Review format with manager to ensure that organization is meeting guidelines.
Use minutes guidelines for preparation of minutes.	3/25	Are minutes accurate and prepared within deadline?	Meet with secretary to review minutes guidelines. (Will secretary attend and take notes?)

that can be used in transferring skills to the workplace. The reality is that evaluation works best as part of the training design. It takes time to plan and should be considered part of the overall training design.

Now that we have reviewed the basics of creating successful training, we turn our attention to the key issues of training and organizational development and the training professionals. In Chapter Seven, we review obstacles to training and ways to overcome them.

Exhibit 6.4 Sample Learning Contract (or Learning Log)

For each week, complete the following log:

Training program: Recognition Secrets

Learning goals: Learn ten new ways to recognize staff.

Develop plan for departmental recognition.

What are the three actions you took this week in support of your learning goals?

1. Identified and implemented recognition with three new employees.

2. Discussed recognition as part of this week's staff meeting agenda.

3. Developed a recognition planner for each staff member.

What are the lessons you have learned (the "aha's"), based on your goals?

Power of recognition—how much staff appreciates recognition.

What is your focus for next week?

Implementing more recognition secrets.

Obstacles to Training and Ways to Overcome Them

If we were to poll health care trainers on the challenges they face, the list might include these three:

1. Managers know that their employees need training yet tell you that the training program can only last forty-five minutes.

2. Senior management tells you there's no money in the budget for training.

3. Staff are on their shift and taking care of patients; supervisors know that some skills need refinement, yet the staff can't attend a training session in a classroom.

These represent some of the unique challenges and obstacles faced by today's health care trainers. In this chapter, we review the common obstacles and challenges familiar to health care trainer colleagues across the country. They include budget constraints, time constraints, lack of creative alternatives to classroom training, and misunderstandings about what training can accomplish. As a health care trainer, I have built my career on learning to deal effectively with challenges of this sort. I know that how these obstacles are handled often has an impact on the credibility of the trainer.

Let me give you an example. Jennifer, a nursing unit manager, recently asked me to conduct team training for her entire unit, more than one hundred employees. She said they were not working together, especially between the day and evening shift. Before committing to the project, I took time to learn if this was a training issue or a performance issue. In other words, did the staff not work together because they did not know how to work cooperatively, or was it because they were not aware of their supervisor's expectations, or because they were not rewarded for working together? Good training assessment questions and careful analysis revealed that the employees did know how to work together. In fact, they were actually rewarded for *not* being supportive of each other—and here is how.

The day shift did not want to accept admissions right before the end of the shift because this would require them to stay late. Instead, they left these admissions for the evening shift to pick up their work. In essence, by not working together the day shift was "rewarded" by being able to go home a little bit earlier.

We look at this example more in depth in this chapter, but for now it illustrates that training is not an appropriate solution to this sort of problem.

The focus of this chapter is how to provide training appropriately and how to handle the challenges that come when managers want training and you know that it won't work. This issue affects a trainer's credibility. As a practitioner, I feel it is my obligation to ensure that the work I do adds value and achieves the results my clients want. However, I have to work to identify the best solutions for the performance problem, and not just what the client thinks he needs.

Trainers can fall into a cycle of trying to meet their clients' needs while knowing that the obstacles the clients also present may negatively influence the quality of training delivered. Understanding the major obstacles and developing suitable alternatives may help to counter such effects. The most common obstacles and challenges are:

- Lack of money or budget for training
- Lack of time for training
- Unrealistic requests
- Lack of creative alternatives to classroom training
- Misunderstanding among senior executives and the organization about what training can accomplish

LACK OF MONEY OR BUDGET FOR TRAINING

One of the major obstacles facing health care trainers is lack of budget or funds for quality training. Health care has traditionally been behind the curve when it comes to dollars spent for training activities. In a recent ASTD benchmarking study, it was noted that although health care has the highest percentage of employees who are trained, it has the lowest training expenditure per employee and the lowest percentile of training dollars as a percentage of payroll (ASTD, 1998 Benchmarking Service). Additionally, in the past the orientation of training has been clinical, which is often less expensive to fund.

Now, as health care seeks to redefine itself, training is expanding to include broader topics such as management and leadership development, customer service, and other soft skills. This type of training is often expensive and difficult to fund and justify. Leaders may not necessarily see the benefits of training. The assumption is that leadership development, customer service, and communication skills can be conducted in the same way and at the same cost as clinical education. Unfortunately, this is not always the case.

Few health care organizations understand the cost of providing training. Many do not budget for staff to attend training. One of the key roles of the health care trainer is to educate his organization on the cost of training and to provide methods to show a return on the investment. This is especially important for the so-called soft skills.

There are several ways to estimate the cost of training. One well-known model is in the work of Jack Phillips. His *Handbook of Training Evaluation and Measurement Methods* proposes several methods to use in developing a cost analysis for training programs, as well as other ways to measure the cost and return on investment of training programs. Normally, it is important to include everything: the trainer's salary, the length of time for designing the program, the participants' hourly rate, the cost of materials, square footage, and refreshments. Exhibit 7.1 is a sample of what you need to consider in developing a cost analysis.

The key is to develop a cost-per-person figure for the proposed training. This helps justify the budget needed to conduct training. It also helps managers determine whether training is a cost-effective solution to organizational problems. Let's look at an example.

Ann, a clinical educator, has been asked to develop a four-hour workshop on EKGs for twenty clerks in an administrative unit in nursing. The program sponsor

Exhibit 7.1 Sample Cost Analysis

Design	Cost
Conducting needs assessment (NA) • Trainer's hourly rate x hours spent in NA	
Designing training content material • For each hour of instruction, three hours of trainer's time (_____ hours x trainer's hourly rate) • Administrative assistant's time; for each hour of instruction, 1.5 hours of administrative time (_____ hours of instruction x 1.5 x administrative assistant hourly rate)	
Material cost • Participant materials per set (copying cost) • Video rentals (cost) • Extra supplies (cost)	
Delivery • Delivery (trainer's hourly rate x number of hours to deliver)	
Participant's cost • Average participant's hourly rate x number of hours of workshop	
Facilities rental • Space and equipment cost	
Refreshments • Cost	
Evaluation • Evaluation cost (trainer hourly rate x number of hours to conduct)	
TOTAL To get cost per participant, divide total cost by number of participants	

is the vice president of nursing. The purpose of the program is to train the clerks on how to perform an EKG; the perceived benefit is to develop a cost-effective delivery system for conducting EKGs on clients. As part of the overall training design, Ann prepares a cost analysis (Exhibit 7.2) to let her client, the vice president of nursing, know what the cost of the training will be.

As you can see, the cost per participant is $246. When the nursing VP considers the potential value of unit clerks being able to perform an EKG and the actual cost of the program, she realizes that her return on a training investment is not high. Therefore, she decides to consider other delivery methods to meet her staffing needs.

Exhibit 7.2 Sample Cost Analysis for One Four-Hour EKG Training Program for Twenty Participants

Design cost:

Trainer's hourly rate ($20) x 20 hours of preparation	=	$400
Materials and equipment:		
Participant workbooks	=	200
EKG monitors	=	200
Video rental	=	100

Delivery:

Trainer hourly rate ($20) x 4 hours	=	80
Average participant's hourly rate ($15) x 4 hours	=	1,200
Refreshments for _____ session(s)	=	180
Facilities rental for _____ session(s)	=	120

Evaluation:

Mentor $20 per hour per 5 participants x 8 hours	=	640
Participant's hourly rate ($15) x 8 hours	=	1,200
Equipment	=	500
Evaluation and competency validation	=	100
TOTAL COST	=	$4,920
Cost divided by 20 participants	=	$246

Cost analysis is an important consideration for today's health care trainer. As resources grow limited, this type of analysis affords trainers and their clients a clear idea of the cost associated with training, as well as assisting in quantifying the benefits or results of training. I find this analysis also helps justify the training expenditure. I use it as a tool to educate senior leaders on the cost associated with the delivery of training and, at the same time, identify how and where we should continue to invest our resources.

LACK OF TIME FOR TRAINING

"I have forty-five minutes. Can you teach customer service or communication skills?"

"I need this training, and I need it tomorrow!"

Trainers often receive unrealistic requests of this type, usually without full appreciation of the basic components of training such as the design and development of the program, materials, evaluation, and measurement. One of the major mistakes that trainers make is to react immediately to such a request and not first evaluate it.

As a new trainer, I fell victim to this all the time. I reacted to the customer's need; I was eager to give them what they wanted. As I learned more about training and development, I learned to try to work with the client to help them understand the requirements of the training request and suggest suitable alternatives.

The most important component of the trainer's role is to spend the time up front to determine whether or not training is the right solution. If a manager has forty-five minutes for customer-service training, it makes sense to conduct a problem analysis to first determine if training is the appropriate solution. If training is the answer, the trainer can then present a plan that includes expected cost, time, and goals, as well as the expected outcomes. This is better use of the manager's and trainer's time than just responding with a generic program.

If a manager insists on training, there may be several ways to accomplish the training within the required time frame. Sometimes it helps to redirect the training request to a specific skill that can actually be conducted within the allotted time. For example, when confronted with a request for, say, a one-hour customer service training session, I focus the training on one skill, such as how to ask a patient for feedback or how to answer the telephone properly. The key is to help managers find solutions to their needs or performance problems.

LACK OF CREATIVE SOLUTIONS TO CLASSROOM TRAINING

As the health care environment changes, there is a need to develop creative alternatives to classroom training. Health care has typically not engaged in other training technologies, such as online or web-based training, to deliver what is required. As resources continue to dwindle, there is an ever-greater need to explore options outside the traditional classroom-training approach.

In my health care organization, short staffing and dwindling revenues have limited the ability of managers and staff to attend classroom training. In clinical areas, for example, along with the cost of sending a staff member to a session, there are additional costs for replacement workers. This trend has given us incentives to rethink how we will continue to offer training in the future. We have recently purchased a computer-based training system to allow us to deliver the mandatory skills training directly to the employees' worksite.

CD-ROMs and CBT are alternatives available to teach everything from management skills to basic dysrhythmias. Other methods include job aids, or an easy-to-use format that explains the steps and procedures in a process, such as a check sheet with instructions on how to complete documentation on a calorie count check. Typically, these alternatives require less time and fewer resources, while providing training when it is convenient for the trainee and manager. Here is a summary of methods that can be considered alternatives to classroom training:

- Self-directed training: completed by the participant, often alone, without instruction.

- Developmental assignments: learning assignments that are completed as part of a job assignment. Preparation of a budget.

- CD-ROMs: courses that are developed and completed via CD-ROM. Interaction often occurs through making choices or taking action.

- CBT: training completed via computer.

- Job aids: tools that can be used for teaching and references, such as a laminated card with operating instructions for a monitor.

- Demonstration: task or competence demonstrated to participant. Often requires return demonstration. Can the learner demonstrate ability to perform it (say, demonstrate how to clean a patient's room)?

MISUNDERSTANDING WHAT TRAINING CAN ACCOMPLISH

One of the common challenges trainers face is helping an organization understand what training is and is not. Training is a means of resolving a performance problem and changing behavior. This may involve gaining awareness or understanding of a skill, applying the knowledge to learning a skill, and changing an attitude or value using a variety of learning methods.

Training is frequently viewed as an answer to any and every performance problem. Sometimes it seems that whenever there is a problem, the call goes out for training. I have received training requests for everything from "My employee is rude to patients and needs customer-service training" to "Employees in my department don't get along; they need to learn to work as a team—could you come and do a one-hour session on teamwork?" When training is perceived as the answer to these problems, it is often prescribed without clear understanding of the actual problem. Someone once described it as "'car-wash training': we run people through it, and then they're fixed or cleaned."

Here is a method for helping clients understand whether or not training is the correct way to resolve their performance problem.

PROBLEM ANALYSIS

One of the ways to overcome this obstacle is to clarify when training is the appropriate solution. The first step is to make the problem evident. What is really going on? That is, what is occurring that leads the manager to suppose that training is required?

Take the example of a manager whose employee is rude to patients. A trainer needs to act as a detective to discover the underlying problem. Necessary questions include: What actually happened? How does the manager define *rude?* What specific things is the employee doing or not doing that lead the manager to assume that the employee is rude to patients? Does the employee know the expectations regarding dealing with patients? Can the employee interact with patients appropriately? These questions serve to generate data that help the trainer identify solutions. Take, for example, the question dealing with expectations. If the employee does not know what is expected regarding patient interaction, then this is a necessary starting place, as opposed to assuming that the employee is rude because of a skill deficiency.

These questions represent the beginning of problem analysis. This is a useful tool in my training and organizational development practice. Problem analysis is a process that can be used to determine the true issue or problem and its likely causes. Clarifying the scope of the problem facilitates finding an appropriate solution.

Let's return to our example. The employee was rude to patients on three occasions, and the manager has failed to discuss the problem with the employee. Instead of automatically instituting a training solution, the trainer should put the responsibility back on the manager. The manager should set expectations for patient interactions ("You need to introduce yourself when you enter the patient's room," or "You need to ask the patient what she needs pleasantly and courteously"). In addition, the manager needs to establish the consequences for continued poor performance. This approach may take longer and produce more work for the manager, but it leads to a productive solution.

For purposes of conducting a problem analysis, there are some common questions:

1. What is currently happening? Describe current performance.

2. What should be happening? Describe the desired performance.

3. What is the performance gap? Identify causes.

- Skill: Do people know what to do? If their job depended on it, could they do it?

- Timing: How often do they have to perform the task?

- Disincentives: Are there any disincentives for correct performance (for example, more work)?

- Rewards: Are they rewarded for not performing (say, less work)?

- Consequences: What are the consequences for no performance?

- Barriers: What are the barriers to performance?

4. What training has been provided? How long ago?

5. What is the cost of poor performance?

Now let's look at using this problem analysis in action to determine whether training is the appropriate solution.

Debbie, a training specialist, received a call from Roxanne, the manager of the Pediatric Nursing Unit. Roxanne asks Debbie to run a time management program for her nursing staff. Roxanne informs Debbie that her day shift has not been able recently to complete their assignments, and they are leaving them for the afternoon shift. In addition, the day shift people are often not able to admit patients at the end of the shift, and they are well behind in the work assignments. Roxanne feels that the staff needs to learn how to manage time better to ensure prompt completion of assignments.

Using the problem-analysis questions, Debbie analyzes the request:

1. What is currently occurring?

- Tasks aren't completed on time. The nurses are leaving work such as baths for the next day. They know how to complete the task; they do it on days when there is a low patient census. When there are callouts or high census, they have a difficult time getting their work done.

2. What should be happening?

- The nurses should complete all the tasks that are assigned to the shifts, including charting on patients and baths.

3. What is the performance, and what are the causes of the gap?

- Skill: the nurses know how to complete their assignment; they have demonstrated this ability on days when there is a low patient census.
- Timing: they perform these duties every day.
- Disincentives for correct performance: none. There are no disincentives for doing the job correctly.
- Rewards for nonperformance: yes. They get to go home on time.
- Consequences: none. The 3:00–11:00 P.M. shift will complete their assignments.
- Barriers: none.
- Training: there has been no formal training on time management.
- Cost of poor performance: one cost is that the day shift has caused some hard feelings with the other shifts, which has had an impact on the unit's operations.

After the analysis, Debbie concludes training is not the best solution and works with Roxanne to develop a plan for the day shift that requires them to complete all tasks before they go home, as well as a change in schedules to accommodate these tasks.

As this case illustrates, problem analysis helps Debbie identify the best solution for Roxanne. This process can be somewhat time consuming, but it's worth it to determine the right solution to the right problem.

POSTTRAINING COMPETENCE

Another component of this issue is lack of understanding of the difference between training and performance. Trainers can aid skill development, but they cannot ensure that trainees are able to perform the skill on the job; that is the manager's responsibility. The manager needs to promote effective performance by allowing the employee a chance to practice newly acquired skills. Just sending the employee to training does not automatically ensure performance.

In one instance, a manager had an employee who was unable to meet a clinical competency requirement of drawing blood. The manager sent the employee to the phlebotomy training program a second time. The employee still failed to meet the competency requirement, and the manager was angry and questioned the value of training ("I sent her through training twice, why is she still not consistently competent?"). The manager mistakenly assumed that by simply sending his employee through phlebotomy training twice, she would be competent to draw blood.

In a situation like this, the manager needs coaching. This might include reviewing the training program outline and developing a plan to reinforce successful performance. The manager may want to watch the employee draw blood and offer feedback on technique. The manager needs to eliminate obstacles to successful performance. As the employee is beginning to draw blood from patients, she should not be given patients from whom it is difficult to draw blood, such as infants, children, and elderly patients. From this example, it is apparent that the manager plays a vital part in maximizing training effectiveness, and the trainer needs to clearly delineate the role of training.

ABLE TO, WILLING TO, ALLOWED TO

When I consider an employee's performance of his job, I am always wondering, "Does the employee have the skills and knowledge to perform the job (is he *able to* do it)? Is the employee motivated to perform the job (is he *willing to* do it)? Is he given the resources and the necessary environment to perform the job (is he *allowed to* do it)?

Training should be used only in the case of employees not knowing something that they need to know to do their job, not to deal with other motivational or circumstantial issues. If, for instance (using our chapter example), a nurse refuses to accept a patient at change of shift, the manager may request she attend training to become a better team player. However, in exploring the problem, if it appears that by refusing a patient assignment at change of shift the nurse finishes work thirty minutes earlier, this is a motivation issue and not a training problem. The nurse will benefit from better understanding the consequences of shirking responsibility, which is most likely to have an impact on her willingness to do the job.

One way I help managers understand the difference is to ask, "If the employees' lives were threatened, would they know how to do this?" Although the question seems a bit melodramatic, it does help illustrate training versus performance. If the employee can perform under any circumstance, this may well be a motivational or circumstantial issue better not handled with training. If the answer to the question is no—the employee cannot perform under any circumstance—then you have a training issue and the trainer can prescribe training with confidence.

It takes courage and confidence for the trainer to educate the organization as to correct applications of training. Analyzing the motivation factors and the entire context of the job, as well as the skill performance of the employee, rather than simply doing training for training's sake, can increase productivity, decrease costs, and strengthen the trainer's role in the health care organization.

CONCLUSION

We have explored the common challenges and obstacles faced by today's health care trainers. In particular, we looked at budget constraints, time constraints, lack of creative alternatives to classroom training, and misunderstandings about what training can accomplish; we addressed how trainers are handling these challenges. We looked at how trainers can respond to these issues with such tools as cost analysis, problem identification, and performance analysis. These obstacles continue to affect trainers, but with careful analysis and a strong commitment to creating solutions that lead to results health care trainers can proceed to meet these challenges head on.

In the next chapter, we show you how to manage your career success in health care training.

You as a Resource: Positioning Yourself for Success

Trainers who focus solely on educational programs often do not provide optimal service to their organizations. Their focus is on the challenges of providing in-services and determining which "generic programs" would be good for their employees to attend. This focus is important, but it represents a past way to view the training professional's role. Today's health care trainers have the opportunity to position themselves in leadership roles, and to position their organizations for success in the new millennium.

In this chapter, we look at several techniques that help you position yourself for success. They include continuous learning, knowing the core business of your organization, and developing a consulting mind-set. I review the last two techniques in depth, with the understanding that some readers may not yet be involved in consulting. Your job and your interest is in becoming a top-notch training professional—as it should be. Nevertheless, I feel certain that you will find links from this new context to some of the training basics we discussed earlier in Chapters Three through Six. In addition, you will find the material interesting and useful in broadening your concept of training and development.

THE PATH TO SUCCESS

Let's begin by looking at one trainer's plan for success and then continue with a discussion of each topic.

Jane is a new director of training and development for a university teaching hospital. She wants to position herself for success and also wants to create a department that adds value to the hospital's strategic business plan and the effectiveness of its workforce. She develops a strategy.

First, she spends time getting to know the hospital and its operational goals and objectives. She takes time to learn the key business initiatives and objectives so that she can link the training-and-development programs directly to these objectives. In fact, she even conducts a needs assessment to ensure that the managers and staff have the right skills to achieve the organizational results.

Second, she begins to position her department and staff in the role of internal consultant. She invests in consulting-skills training for the training specialists and begins to proactively look for opportunities where training can serve as a critical component of any initiatives. With her staff, she partners with senior management to identify appropriate training and organizational development interventions that support key hospital initiatives. She is thinking outside the traditional training box.

Jane also remains current in the field of training and organizational development. She is active in the local chapter of the ASTD. She reads journals and books and attends professional development meetings to increase her knowledge of training and identify ways she can continue to link training trends to her own organization.

As this example illustrates, Jane is purposeful in developing strategies to position herself and her department as key contributors to organizational success. In a time of continued reduction of resources, these techniques have ensured that the training-and-development department is seen as a value-added service; they have helped health care training professionals around the country continue to have the resources necessary to meet their organization's challenges.

Continuous Learning

Learn, learn, learn. Both the world of training and the business of health care are changing rapidly, so it is important to stay abreast of current realities and future challenges. Continuous learning allows trainers to analyze how trends and challenges are affecting their organization as well as seek ways to address these concerns. Some of the best sources for such information include ASTD and the American Hospital Association (AHA). Both organizations have terrific journals that provide up-to-the-minute information. In addition, ASTD has local chapters throughout the country where one can learn about the training field, as well as take advantage of annual conferences.

Other great sources are books and journals in the field of leadership and management. I read a great deal and try to keep up with the major trends in these areas. Then I spend time thinking about their application to health care, and in particular to my own organization.

It is very important to take time to plan your career. You may be a clinical practitioner new to training-and-development methodologies and principles. If so, ask yourself: "How will I transfer my skill and knowledge to a larger learning organization?" "How will I begin to learn new competencies and training theories as I take on new roles in training and employee development?"

My suggestion is to develop your own learning strategy by talking to your manager, and by conducting informational interviews with training professionals within your department and in other organizations. Ask them to describe the high-priority competencies for a trainer in health care. Find out how they learn and practice key competencies in their work. Observe your colleagues as they teach courses, whether similar to your own course load or entirely new. Consider finding a training mentor; better yet, become a health care mentor to an experienced trainer who is new to the health care setting.

If you are a seasoned trainer or consultant, ask yourself, "How will I learn more about transferring my expertise to a health care environment?" Then apply some of my prior suggestions to your learning plan.

Lastly, benchmarking also yields wonderful ideas and suggestions on how leading organizations are responding to trends with creative solutions. In particular, I look outside of health care to leaders in other industries and in companies such as Sears, General Electric, and Motorola. These organizations are not only successful but are also doing cutting-edge work in the areas of training and organizational development.

Knowing the Core Business

Health care leaders are well versed in their organizational business strategy. Trainers should be no exception. Trainers should learn about the business of health care and also understand the key management and financial measures of success. In addition, they should be familiar with the organizational business strategy. Two ways to accomplish this include studying the organization's strategic plan and talking to senior managers about their goals and objectives. I often start out conversations by asking: "What are your business goals?" "What things keep you awake at night?" "What are the three major things that we need to accomplish this year?" This gives me insight into their key concerns and helps me to proactively identify learning applications and solutions. Furthermore, by focusing on business needs, I as a trainer can link training to the health care organization's business objectives and strategic plan.

One of the best tools I have developed to show the linkage between training and the business of a medical center is developing a training or learning strategic plan based on an organizational business assessment. This plan identifies recommendations founded on key issues or themes that a trainer uncovers by asking questions such as those in the preceding paragraph. Exhibit 8.1 is a sample page from such a plan, which focuses on the issue of learning organizations.

In this example, you can see that the overall issue or theme is related to learning organizations and there are recommendations that address this issue; there is also an indication of when the recommendation will be completed. Some of the other issues identified include communication, medical staff alignment, performance management, vision and mission, and planning processes. The beauty of a plan like this is that the issues are not typical training program issues but instead presented in a broader organizational context.

Let me share briefly how I develop this type of learning strategy. Note that this process has similarities to the training needs assessment we reviewed in Chapter Three. This organizational assessment differs primarily in the focus of the questions, and oftentimes in the level of those interviewed. Let's begin.

Step One. Conduct interviews, assessment, and focus groups that review the key business and organizational issues. Some of the questions that I ask are:

Exhibit 8.1 Sample Training Strategic Plan

Learning Organizations

Issue: Currently, there is no continuous and enhanced capacity to learn, adapt, and change. Learning is not viewed as a key strategic skill; as an organization, we do not engage in processes of purposeful learning.

Recommendations

Profile the system's learning capacity and determine focus areas (first quarter).

Build dialogue into processes (for example, post mortem: ask questions such as what worked and what did not work) and into key operational and strategic processes (second quarter).

Create organizational cross-functional learning teams and a self-learning network. This begins at the management level; senior management will lead (third quarter).

Develop a learning academy that features learning opportunities for all employees (fourth quarter).

- What are our medical center's strengths and weaknesses?

- Who are our competitors and what are they focusing on?

- What efforts should the training-and-development department focus on in the next six months?

- What do you need your managers and employees to focus on or develop in the next year?

In addition to assessments, I also review the organization's financial reports. In understanding how the organization makes money, the trainer increases credibility when communicating the current realities of the organization. Other sources of data to review include quality information, benchmarking or best-practice information, and staffing and customer-service data.

Step Two. Summarize data into an observation statement. I review all of the information that was collected and identify statements that reflect the information ("Employees do not understand the strategic plan"). I normally put these statements on index cards for easy sorting.

Step Three. After creating statements, I sort them into themes and categories. In this example, *learning organization* was identified as one of the themes.

Step Four. From the themes, create issue statements. These should be stated in the organizational context of why they are important. In the learning organization theme, the issue is: "Currently, there is not a continuous and enhanced capacity to learn, adapt, and change. Learning is not viewed as a key strategic skill, and as an organization we do not engage in processes of purposeful learning."

Step Five. Develop recommendations that respond to the issue. The recommendation should answer the questions *who, when,* and *where.* One of the recommendations is to "develop a learning academy that will feature learning opportunities for all employees" (as cited earlier in the sample training strategic plan of Exhibit 8.1).

Developing a learning strategy affords me the opportunity to align the processes of my training-and-development functions with the core business needs of the organization. The plan not only increases my credibility as an organizational leader by proactively supporting the organization; it helps cement the value added by training.

Additionally, by examining core businesses of the organization, you as a trainer can gain a complete picture of the organization so as to present it, when appropriate, as a solution to a business need. If the core business need is to deliver quality patient care faster and more efficiently, then linking a clinical competency such as phlebotomy as the means to this goal gives this training effort high importance. If one of the business goals is to increase the morale of the employees, then training on recognition or motivation may be appropriate. In all cases, training should be linked to all business needs or the strategic plan.

Developing a Consultant Mind-Set

One of the best ways to position yourself for success is to develop a consultant mind-set. As a consultant, your emphasis shifts from solely improving individual performance to addressing performance at the individual, team, and organizational levels. As I discussed earlier in the book, for trainers this may mean a transition from prescribing training as a solution to addressing performance through a variety of interventions.

On any given day, I am asked to consult on a variety of learning and performance issues that may include, say, coaching a manager on how to build a team, planning a strategic planning retreat, or mediating a dispute between two employees. In this type of assignment, I typically intervene in a system or workgroup to help change behavior or performance. Interventions can take many forms: strategic planning; meditation; work redesign; job aids; and designing and developing vision, mission, and values. It is important to note that these interventions may or may not include training. They often involve partnering with managers and employees to identify a need, create a solution, and develop accountabilities.

For consulting efforts to be successful, the trainer must use good consulting skills (many of which build on the solid facilitation skills of attending, questioning, and listening), needs assessments, and evaluation skills, as discussed earlier. In other words, good consulting skills build on good trainer skills. The consulting process consists of the steps shown in Figure 8.1: entry and contracting, data collection and diagnosis, client feedback and design of interventions, conducting interventions, and evaluation.

Step One: Entry and Contracting. Step one is the first meeting with the person who has requested the work, or the client. At this initial meeting, the client gives an overview of the problem or issue and states the goals of the project. Take time to ask questions to gain a clear picture of what the problem and the issues are. This initial phase of the working relationship is very important and often sets the stage for developing rapport and comfort with the client.

In addition to the client's goals, it is important for the consultant to impart an overview of the methods of data collection, what happens with the information,

Figure 8.1 The Consulting Model

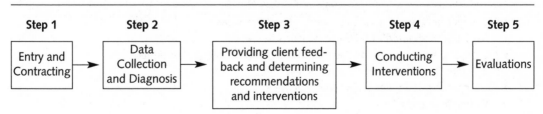

Step 1	Step 2	Step 3	Step 4	Step 5
Entry and Contracting	Data Collection and Diagnosis	Providing client feedback and determining recommendations and interventions	Conducting Interventions	Evaluations

the amount of time it takes, and what is expected of the client. These components are reviewed in later steps. It is also important to clarify the consultant's role in the project.

The contracting meeting can be summarized in a written document called a "statement of understanding" or contract. This written summary lays out the stated goals, the proposed plan and time lines, and any boundaries or parameters. A good statement of understanding includes the specifics of the organizational development plan, as well as roles and responsibilities. Additionally, the statement of understanding may offer examples of the type of data to be collected as well as any project deliverables.

Exhibit 8.2 is a sample of a statement of work that I used in a consulting assignment. In this example, note that I spell out the proposed needs, outcomes, the approach that I will be using, and cost and time estimates.

Exhibit 8.2 Sample Statement of Understanding

Date: February 22, 2000

To: Dr. John Doe

From: Jane Smith, Director, Training and Organization Development, XYZ Hospital

Re: Departmental Team Building

This memo outlines how I believe I can best help you and your staff in your continuing journey to build a more productive working team. Based on the meeting with the faculty group, I am convinced they are ready to take on this type of effort.
The proposal is discussed under the following headings:

    I.   Preliminary understanding of need
    II.   Desired outcomes
    III. Overall approach
    IV.   Cost estimate

I. Preliminary Understanding of Need
I understand that the department has experienced several problems over the past few years:

- Conflict between the manager and some employees
- Lack of coordinated or integrated efforts in serving the hospital
- Lack of ownership among the employee group for the performance and direction of the department as a whole
- Interpersonal conflicts between employees
- Conflicting goals
- Perceived inequalities in workloads and work assignments

II. Desired Outcomes

The department wishes to accomplish several outcomes:

- Clear definition of and commitment to operating norms
- Developing the department into a high-performing team
- Better relationship among all members of the department
- Alignment on goals and direction of the department

There appears to be a chronic aspect to the issues you presented when we met. That is, there are some well-entrenched patterns at work in the group. My experience is that organizations, groups, and individuals tend to cover the same ground over and over until they:

1. Come to understand the patterns of performance
2. Commit to a vision of what they want to create
3. Work to move beyond current and past limitations into developing new operating norms that include acquiring any new information, skills, and resources needed
4. Put their strategies into action by positioning themselves for opportunities, through a careful planning and measurement process

III. Proposed Approach

The overall approach has several major components:

- Assessing department and employee group and individual patterns of behavior and their impact on the effectiveness of the department, including development of the department's culture profile
- Development of a common vision for the department (i.e., what are the results you want to create, and to what end?)
- Team building with the department; developing operational guidelines (norms, feedback mechanism, etc.)

This approach includes:

- Individual interviews with all employees
- Individual and group assessment
- Analysis and report, using some data from interviews and observations
- Feedback to the employee group
- Development of specific interventions (team building, coaching, etc.)

IV. Cost Estimate

The cost for the first phase of this project—which includes the individual interviews, individual and group assessments, analysis and report, and feedback to the group—is $1,000 plus any material costs that may be incurred. In addition, as we move into developing specific interventions, I will give you the estimated cost prior to proceeding.

Conclusion

I am excited about the opportunity to work with you and your staff. As you described them, the group is bright; I think they are willing to devote the time and energy to reach their potential as a team. I would be happy to discuss this plan with you or provide any additional information. I look forward to hearing from you.

The statement of understanding should be reviewed with the client for agreement and understanding. Sometimes obtaining a signature for approval is a good way to establish the seriousness of the agreement.

The biggest factors in the success of the consulting project are encountered in this entry or contracting phase. Some of the most common issues include lack of commitment on the client's part and unclear expectations about the outcome. In both of these instances, the consultant must return to the contract and clarify the client's role. In some cases, a frank discussion is needed to ensure understanding and commitment. If the commitment is not there, the consultant should consider not proceeding.

Step Two: Data Collection and Diagnosis. Normally, the consultant uses a variety of data collection methods to develop a full picture of the problems or issue. It is important to hear from the entire team about the perception of the issues and concerns. Just as data collection is vital in designing a training program, so is it critical for successful diagnosis of the problem. It helps ensure that the intervention or action is appropriate. Here are a variety of ways I use to collect data. Again, you will note some overlap of this material with that in Chapter Three on needs assessment.

Individual Interviews. Although the individual interview is often the preferred method (since it permits confidentiality of data), it can be costly. It takes more time to interview every group member individually. Restating or paraphrasing, asking questions, and encouraging the interviewee help the consultant gain information. To ensure consistency, she may develop an interview guide (prepared in advance) to record information.

Individual interview questions should be open-ended. Questions should also be followed up with additional probing for more information. Here are some excerpts from an interview guide that I used in a consulting assignment with a nursing unit. The assignment focused on increasing team effectiveness. In this example, the questions are open-ended and cover a wide range of issues.

Sample Nursing Unit Interview Guide
- What do you consider to be the strengths of the Nursing Unit?
- What do you like best about working in the unit?

- What do you find most frustrating about working in the unit?

- What are some operational issues and barriers to effective functioning or more effective team work?

- What are some old or recurring problems or issues that get in the way of your positive support?

- What contributions you are willing to make to improve the situation?

- How can management help (especially Mary _____ or Dr. Smith)?

Focus Groups. Focus groups are group interviews. They work well if there are a large number of people involved in data collection and if time constraints prevent individual interviews. However, they often do not produce the same level of honest feedback because people may be uncomfortable in front of others. Running a focus group takes preparation and planning.

Here are some guidelines to consider in developing effective interviews and focus groups.

Interviews

- Begin with an overview of the process.

- Keep information confidential.

- Use open-ended questions to encourage the interviewee.

- Summarize information to ensure complete understanding.

Think of an interview as peeling an onion. Start with general questions and then move in on the specifics; as an example, "Describe your team. . . . Tell me how your team communicates. . . . Give me examples of how the team manages conflict."

Focus Groups

1. Prepare in advance.

- Introduce the focus group members—by first name only.

- Review why you are holding the focus group, your role, and confidentiality.

2. Give the ground rules.

- Everyone needs to participate.

- Keep the focus on the topic.
- It's OK to disagree.
- Be open and honest.
- Questions should go from general to specific.

3. Ask each individual to respond to the same questions.

Assessments. Assessments are another way of collecting data. Surveys and questionnaires can be completed individually to explore key issues. There are many assessments on the market targeted on a variety of issues, such as communication or team effectiveness. In a team-building project, a team effectiveness profile could be used to show individual and group perceptions on diverse criteria of team effectiveness.

In determining a plan for data collection, it is important to understand what type of information needs to be collected. It is often a good idea to use the client's perspective of the problem to begin. Sue, a nursing manager, asks for help in improving the effectiveness of her nursing team. Exhibit 8.3 is a sample plan for data collection on team effectiveness.

Alongside data collection, the second component to this step is actual diagnosis of the problem. The consultant needs to review the data collected and arrive at a diagnosis concerning the problem, as well as recommendations for action. He

Exhibit 8.3 Sample Plan for Data Collection on Team Effectiveness (2–Blue Unit)

Objective: Sue, the manager, wants to increase the effectiveness of the 2–blue unit.

- Increase and improve interpersonal communication between shifts.
- Increase shared leadership on unit teams and committees.
- Increase input, and develop plan for improvement.

Based on these goals, the OD consultant, Matt, developed the following plan:

- Interviews with managers and assistant nurse managers.
- Focus group with staff members.
- Review patient satisfaction (or employee satisfaction) data instrument and team communication profiles.

---

should have an unbiased view of the data and develop a recommended course of action. Ultimately, it is up to the client to determine what actions to take.

Step Three: Feedback and Design of Interventions. After data collection and diagnosis, the consultant needs to determine a process for giving feedback or the results of the effort to the client. It is important for the consultant to be diplomatic in the feedback process. The client normally becomes somewhat defensive about the data, especially if they challenge the manager's style or the organization's usual practices.

In preparing the feedback, consider organizing the data thematically, with like responses grouped together around distinct and clearly defined issues. These themes may include communication, leadership, systems structure, performance, and rewards. In presenting the feedback to the client, it is also important to respect anonymity of sources. Typically, the best safeguard for ensuring confidentiality is to make sure the data do not contain any names or direct references. In presenting the information, you should follow a simple five-step meeting plan:

1. Begin with a review of the contract and problem.

2. Review the data-collection methods.

3. Present a summary of the data. (Exhibit 8.4 shows some of the data that was presented to the client, the facilities department.)

4. Present the recommendation.

5. Reach agreement with the client on how to proceed.

As you see, the summary report includes exact quotes from those interviewed. This is important so as to show an unbiased report to the client. The final steps begin with a written recommendation report; a sample follows (Exhibit 8.5).

The final step in this written report is presenting it to the client and achieving agreement on how to proceed. Allow the client an opportunity to ask questions about the data or recommendations. As part of the discussion, the client and consultant should agree on a course of action.

Step Four: Conducting the Interventions. Intervention is the step that causes planned change to occur. It is the catalyst for change. Interventions are customized to the specific problem. For example, an intervention to increase team effectiveness might engage in a process of team building. Or in a conflict between

Exhibit 8.4 Partial Sample of Data Summary of a Team Effectiveness Project (for a Facilities Department)

1. Do you feel the team concept in Facilities has increased or decreased the effectiveness of the department?
   - Definitely increased.
   - Increased effectiveness in many ways, but there is still a lot to be increased (i.e., the circles are still not coming together on policies, procedures, and communication).
   - Increased, because people work together.
   - If nothing else, teams have increased awareness of hospital goals, cost awareness, and a *changing attitude* toward productivity.
   - It has greatly increased the effectiveness. Work order requests were as much as eighteen months old when we took over. Except for parts or the inability to get into some areas, we are up to date.

2. What is working best with teams?
   - We can draw on members for their talents and interests. Training works better in small groups.
   - Work performance; being able to do more than one job. Able to feel everything has a better chance of being run right.
   - There is teamwork; things seem to get done quicker.
   - Team leaders.
   - If one person does not know how to do something, someone on the team will take the time to show them how so they can do it after that.
   - The new evaluation process is a good idea which allows the techs to get involved in each other's annual evaluation.
   - Cohesion of the teams; the ability to cooperate with other teams to solve problems and get the jobs done.

3. What are the most frustrating aspects of the team?
   - Everyone wants it *now*. Not enough manpower to keep up with damage. Need to bring up awareness, and it seems the circles could mesh a little better sometimes. But it is getting better.
   - Too much paperwork.
   - Only one person at a time gets off for vacation or deer season.
   - Due to the number of changes (roles, responsibility changes with manager, supervisors, structure), there has never been total buy-in of team concepts. Some of the changes have created hard feelings, which result in lack of interest or only doing what is necessary. This in turn creates problems throughout the three circles. Seems to be a lot of finger pointing instead of concentrating on the main goal of team concepts. The history behind the development of teams, why teams were started, still hinders the growth of teams.
   - With the team concept, we do more of the labor-type work, i.e., plunging toilets, drains, etc.

two individuals, an intervention might consist of a mediated conflict-resolution session. Training is also an intervention that is useful in increasing skill development. Table 8.1 shows some common interventions.

Although the interventions are often done with the client group, it is important to note the role of the consultant in guiding the intervention. The consultant needs to constantly maintain its quality through a careful management process and continuous review of the intervention to ensure problem resolution.

Step Five: Evaluation. As in a training program, there is a need to evaluate the effectiveness of the consulting assignment. Normally, it is important to consider the evaluation as part of the overall project planning process. It needs to be tailored to the intervention and must measure project progress.

The methods of evaluation are similar to those used in training. In measuring team effectiveness, the consultant may choose to have the client group complete a preassessment and a postassessment of overall team effectiveness. The consultant can also look at existing information, such as patient and employee satisfaction data, as indicators of the effectiveness of the project. In addition to these evaluation methods, it is also useful to ask the client for her perception of the effectiveness of the consulting project.

Table 8.1 Chart of Sample Organizational Development Interventions

Intervention	Purpose
Third-party conflict mediation	To resolve issues between two individuals or groups
Team building	To increase effectiveness of individuals to help them resolve leadership or management issues
Strategic plan	To develop clearly understood plan for future of a department or organization
Individual coaching	Increase effectiveness of individuals to help them resolve leadership or management issues
Expectation management	To clarify expectations of managers and employees
Training	To develop specific skills
Assessment (Myers-Briggs)	To provide a forum to allow people to understand and accept individual differences
Organizational design	To improve team or organizational effectiveness

Exhibit 8.5 Recommendation Report (for an OD Project)

Date:
To: Ann Doe, Practice Manager
From: Susan Lynne, Director, Training and Organizational Development
Re: Team-Building Project

This memo is to summarize the issues and recommendations for the Physician Practice office.

Staffing:	Most people perceived the office to be understaffed. With an increase in the volume of patients, the staff feels overwhelmed.
Leadership:	Dr. Floyd and Jean _____ are perceived to be somewhat ineffective as leaders. Both individuals need to be more assertive in handling staff issues and concerns. Dr. Floyd is weak and avoids conflict and dealing with problems and concerns.
Medical practice group (MPG):	There is a lack of consistent direction input from the MPG. The staff is confused about MPG involvement—what the office can handle versus what the MPG can. The office doesn't see the connection between themselves and what goes on in Smithland.
Organization:	The staff feels overwhelmed. There is lack of good coordination between the front and the back office. People feel they cannot adequately perform their jobs.
Morale:	General climate of the office is poor. The nature of the problems includes staffing, organization, etc.
Teamwork:	Group does not function as a high-performing team. There is lack of clarity of roles, etc.

Recommendations

A team-building session was proposed for Tuesday, December 17. Because the office manager is on medical leave for the next few months, we propose postponing the session until her return. In the meantime, we can begin working on the following recommendations:

1. Conduct staffing workflow analysis to determine appropriate staffing levels. The staffing may be appropriate, but the organization and systems need to be revamped and updated. I suggest that someone flowchart the work processes to look for opportunities to redesign the practice.
2. Create guidelines for staffing practices: how do we go about justifying the need for staff? When can Manpower be called? What processes are discontinued in low-staffing situations?
3. Create leadership and management expectations for Dr. Floyd and Jean _____. Survey staff quarterly to look at leadership and management issues. Both could also benefit from leadership development.
4. Reorganize the front area; it needs to be straightened out and organized. The transcriptionist is in the back; she could be moved to the front to help cover phones, etc.
5. Hold monthly staff meetings to identify issues and concerns with the staff and to apply problem solving to issues.
6. Determine the roles and responsibilities of Jean _____, Dr. Floyd, Ann _____, etc., to clarify the issues.
7. Jean _____ and Dr. Floyd need to spend more time being visible as leaders with the staff.
8. Medical Practice Associates needs to clarify its role in the practice. The perception is that the "power" is in Smithland, and therefore _____ does not assume responsibility for fixing the problems that exist.

First, reach agreement with the client or manager on the approach to resolving the issue. This step involves spelling out the roles and responsibilities of the client and consultant, as well as a time frame.

Second, conduct a needs assessment or evaluation of the problem or issue. A needs assessment may include conducting individual or group interviews, or doing a focused survey and a review of related data or information. The idea is to get a complete picture of what the cause of the problem may be.

Third, develop interventions. Developing interventions can entail training or other means of resolving the problem. These interventions may be applied to an individual, a team, a department, or an organization.

Finally, evaluate the intervention. Did the intervention resolve the problem? Has performance improved? What else needs to occur to enable improved performance? Following up again might instigate another consultative cycle. The major emphasis in this approach is to bring about change in the areas of customer satisfaction, employees, operations, and business strategy.

CONCLUSION

As you can see, positioning yourself for success in the health care training field includes various strategies and mind-sets. First and foremost is to gain knowledge and competence in core training skills, and to become knowledgeable about the business, organizational structure, and staffing of health care organizations (Chapter Two).

Along with enhancing these competencies and knowledge, develop a learning plan for yourself to meet immediate job requirements and long-term career goals. Then begin to get involved with various training and organizational development activities in your department, on both the clinical education and employee leadership development sides. Volunteer to assist your chief learning officer in developing the hospital's strategic plan for learning. Observe other colleagues as they facilitate a team-building effort involving administrators and physicians in the gynecology department. Attend professional meetings at ASTD and the AHA.

Explore. Build on what you already know. Grow!

Resources:
A Health Care Trainer's Toolkit

I n this final chapter, we focus on several resources that are available
to trainers. I have tried to identify those resources that I find most
helpful to me as a health care trainer. They are in the areas of professional associations, training resources, books, and videos.

ASSOCIATIONS

The *American Society for Training and Development* (ASTD) is an international
association for training and development practitioners. With more than fifty
thousand members, it provides a vast resource for members. Within the society,
there is a special forum for trainers who work in health care. They put out
a monthly publication called *Training and Development.* In addition, there are
local chapters throughout the country. For more information, contact ASTD at
(703) 683-8100 or consult their website, at www.astd.org.

The *Health Care Education Association* is a national organization for health care trainers. They provide networking opportunities and other resources for health care trainers. For more information, contact them at (888) 298-3861.

The *Organizational Development Network* is a national organization designed for those individuals who practice organizational development. They offer networking opportunities, as well as training and other resources on organizational development. They have an excellent website with information on membership as well as other resources. They can be reached at (973) 763-7337 or at their website (www.odnet.org).

The *International Society of Performance Improvement* is a national organization dedicated to improving productivity and performance in the workplace. One major focus is human performance technology, which is a systematic approach to improving performance and competence using a combination of performance analysis, cause analysis, and intervention selection. They can be reached at (202) 408-7969.

The *American Hospital Association* (AHA) represents about five thousand health care institutions in advocating health care change and reform. AHA provides excellent resources in all aspects of health care. They publish *Hospitals and Health Networks* magazine. In addition, they have forums available in education and human resources. You can reach the AHA at (312) 422-3000 or at their website, www.aha.org.

TRAINING

These resources give an overview of training, particularly the skills of design and delivery. In addition to the books mentioned here, there are several companies with specialty resources for trainers.

Block, Peter. *Flawless Consulting: A Guide to Getting Your Expertise Used.* (2nd ed.) San Francisco: Jossey-Bass/Pfeiffer, 1999.

Deck, Michele. *Instant Teaching Tools for Health Care Educators. Mosby-Year Book.* St. Louis: Mosby, 1998.

Deck, Michele. *More Instant Teaching Tools for Health Care Educators. Mosby-Year Book.* St. Louis: Mosby, 1998.

Forbess-Greene, Sue. *The Encyclopedia of Icebreakers: Structured Activities That Warm Up, Motivate, Challenge, Acquaint, and Energize.* San Francisco: Jossey-Bass/Pfeiffer, 1993.

Francis, Dave, and Don Young. *Improving Work Groups.* San Francisco: Jossey-Bass/Pfeiffer, 1979.

Gaines Robinson, Dana, and James C. Robinson. *Performance Consulting: Moving Beyond Training.* San Francisco: Berrett-Koehler, 1995.

Hale, Judith A. *The Performance Consultant's Fieldbook: Tools and Techniques for Improving Organizations and People.* San Francisco: Jossey-Bass/Pfeiffer, 1998.

Kirkpatrick, Donald L. *Evaluating Training Programs: The Four Levels.* San Francisco: Jossey-Bass/Pfeiffer, 1994.

Lawson, Karen. *Train-the-Trainer: Facilitator's Guide and Trainer's Handbook.* San Francisco: Jossey-Bass/Pfeiffer, 1998.

Pfeiffer, J. William, ed. *The Encyclopedia of Group Activities: 150 Practical Designs for Successful Facilitating.* San Francisco: Jossey-Bass/Pfeiffer, 1989.

Phillips, Jack. *Handbook of Training Evaluation and Measurement Methods.* Houston: Gulf, 1997.

Phillips, Jack J., ed. *In Action: Conducting Needs Assessment.* Washington, D.C.: ASTD, 1995.

Phillips, Jack J., ed. *In Action: Measuring Return on Investment, Volume 1.* Washington, D.C.: ASTD, 1994.

Phillips, Jack J., ed. *In Action: Measuring Return on Investment, Volume 2.* Washington, D.C.: ASTD, 1997.

Pike, Robert W. *Creative Training Techniques.* Minneapolis: Lakewood Books.

Reddy, W. Brendan. *Intervention Skills: Process Consultation for Small Groups and Teams.* San Francisco: Jossey-Bass/Pfeiffer, 1994.

Silberman, Mel. *20 Active Training Programs, Volumes I, II, and III.* San Francisco: Jossey-Bass/Pfeiffer, 1992.

TRAINING PRODUCTS

HRDQ (which stands for *Human Resource Development Quarterly*) provides terrific assessments, games, training programs, and other learning resources for individuals, teams, and organizations. It is available at (800) 633-4533.

HRD Press (human resources development) offers excellent assessments, workshop designs, and training activities in the areas of employee and management development. They can be reached at (800) 822-2801.

Jossey-Bass/Pfeiffer. In addition to books, Jossey-Bass/Pfeiffer offers resources in a host of training-and-development areas. These include instruments, assessments, and workshop designs. They can be reached at (800) 274-4434.

VIDEOS

I have found *American Media Incorporated* (AMI) to be one of the best. Not only is the quality of the videos excellent but AMI has specialty videos in health care on a wide range of management and employee development topics. For more information, contact them at (800) 262-2557.

Other video resources:

CRM Films offers videos in several areas. For more information, contact them at (800) 421-0833.

MedFilms provides videos on topics specific to health care. For information, contact them at (800) 535-5593.

VideoLearning provides videos on a wide range of topics. Their number is (800) 622-3610.

INDEX

C

Career plan, 114, 115. *See also* Professional development

Cartoons, 67

Case studies, 61

Challenges of training, 101–112; cost constraints as, 103–105; lack of alternatives to classroom training as, 106–107; listed, 101, 102; misunderstanding of training-performance relationship as, 107–112; time constraints as, 105–106

Check sheet, 107

Chief learning officer, 7–8

Classroom training: alternatives to, 65–66, 67, 101, 102, 106–107; behavior problems in, 81–82

Client group clinical education, 14

Clinical education unit, 12–13; in integrated structure, 14; in parallel structure, 13–14

Clinical educators, 10, 12; example of, 17–18; roles and responsibilities of, 17–18

Clinical quality reports, as needs assessment data source, 24

Clinical training needs questionnaire, 32, 49–51

Closed-ended questions, 86

Closing of lecture, 61

Coaching, 111, 127

Color, 76

Commitment, client, 122

Communication skills training: interview guide for needs assessment of, 26; training delivery of, 71–72; training design of, 53–54

CD-ROM training, 107

Competencies and competence: comparing requirements of current and future, 41; defined, 36; development of, 41–42; identification of required, 41; individual development planning and, 39, 40; JCAHO requirements for, 41, 43; managerial, 39, 41; for performance review, 39; posttraining performance problems in, 111; recording of, 44; requirements for, by profession, 36, 37; for selection criteria, 37–39; for succession planning, 39; and training, 35–36; training plan development for, 42; uses of, 37–41; validation of, 42. *See also* Skill requirements

Competency assessment, 35–36, 42–44; process of, 42–44; regulatory requirements for, 35–36, 41, 44. *See also* Evaluation; Tests

Computer-assisted radiology, 3

Computer-based training (CBT), 8, 62, 64, 107; vendors of, for mandatory competencies, 64

Computer-generated overhead transparencies, 78

Condition component of learning objectives, 56

Confidentiality, 125

Conflict management training: sample job aid for, 65–66; sample lesson plan for, 58, 59

Conflict mediation, as organizational development intervention, 127

Conscious sedation skill requirements, 37

Consulting, 113, 114, 118–129; client commitment to, 122; data collection step in, 122–125, 129; entry and contracting step in, 119–122, 129; evaluation of, 127, 129; feedback step in, 125, 126, 128, 129; intervention step in, 125, 127, 129; model of, 119; problem diagnosis step in, 122, 124–125, 129; process of, 118–129; project data summary for, 125, 126; project recommendation report for, 125, 128; skills for, 19, 119; steps for, summarized, 129

Content design, 57–58, 59

Content training versus facilitation, 84–85

Continuous learning: for skill development, 37; for training professionals, 19, 113, 114, 115–116, 129; for training professionals, resources for, 131–134

Continuous process improvement, 6, 9

Contract, internal consulting, 120–122

Contracting meeting, 119–120

Conversation, side, 82

Core business assessment, 113, 114, 116–118, 129

Cost analysis for training programs, 103–105

Cost reduction in health care, 4

Cost-effectiveness: of alternatives to classroom training, 65, 101, 106–107; of integrated structure, 15

Course titles, related to JCAHO requirements, 17

CPR learning objectives, 56

Criteria, performance, 56

CRM Films, 134

Cross-functional learning teams, 10, 64

Cue cards, 77

Curriculum design, 57–58

Customer-service skills training: needs assessment for, 29; needs assessment for, in respiratory therapy case study, 32–35; results measures of, 96

D

Data analysis: for needs assessment, 30–31; of qualitative data, 30–31; of quantitative data, 31

Data collection: for consulting project, 122–125, 129; for needs assessment, 25–30, 33–34; statement of, in needs assessment report, 32

Data sources: for needs assessment, 23–25, 33; for organizational assessment, 116–117; statement of, in needs assessment report, 31

Data summary, for internal consulting project, 125, 126

Delivery. *See* Health care delivery trends; Training delivery

Demographics: in needs assessment surveys, 27; in workforce, 6

Demonstrations: as alternative to classroom training, 107; in competency assessment, 43–44; as learning method, 61; props for, 80

Developmental assignments, 107

Diagnosis: with Internet, 8; needs assessment compared to, 21

Diagnosis-related groups, 3

Diagrams, 67

Dietitian skill requirements, 37

Discussions, 60; facilitation skills for, 84–87; side, 82

Distractions, 86–87

Diversity, workforce, 6, 8

Divisional education, 13

Document reviews, 29–30

Documentation of needs assessment, 31–32

Documentation training, 12

E

EKG competency and training: sample cost analysis for, 103–105; sample learning objectives for, 56; tests of, 29

Emergency room skill requirements, 37

Employee or management development training specialists, 12; example of, 18; roles and responsibilities of, 18. *See also* Management development training

Employee or management development unit, 13; in integrated structure, 14; in parallel structure, 13–14. *See also* Management development training

Employee tally, as needs assessment data source, 33

Engagement in learning: adult learners' need for, 58–59, 83; learning methodologies for promoting, 59–64

Evaluation of consulting, 127, 129

Evaluation of training, 69, 89–100; behavior (level-three), 94–95, 96; benefits of, 89–90, 98; follow-up and, 97–100; four-level model of, 90–97; learning (level-two), 93–94; reaction (level-one), 90–92; results (level-four), 95–97; training design and, 69, 99. *See also* Assessments; Competency assessment; Tests

Exceptional performers, 42

Executive overview, in needs assessment report, 31

Exercises, reading and writing, 62

Expectation management training, 127

Eye contact, 74, 85

F

Facial expressions, 74, 85

Facilitation: content training versus, 84–85; skills of, 71, 84–87

Feedback step, in consulting project, 125, 126, 128, 129

Final report of needs assessment, 31–32

Financial reports, review of, 117

Fire safety job aid, 65

First impression, 83

Flawless Consulting (Block), 81

Flexibility, of integrated structure, 15

Flipcharts, 61, 76–77

Focus groups: conducting, 26–27, 123–124; guidelines for, 123–124; for internal consulting project assessment, 123–124; for needs assessment, 26–27, 30; for organizational assessment, 117; pros and cons of, 30; for training transfer evaluation, 95

Follow-up, 97–98, 99, 100

Frames, transparency, 78

G

Games, 60, 75, 80

Games Trainers Play (Scannell), 80

Gap analysis, 23; data and, 23–24

General Electric, 115

George Washington University training-and-development program, 18

Gestures, 73

Grammar and spelling, 69

Graphic flair, of training materials, 67. *See also* Visual aids

Group discussion, 60, 83; facilitation of, 84–87

H

Handbook of Training Evaluation and Measurement Methods (Phillips), 103

Hands-on activities, 75

Health care: trends in, 1–5; workplace trends and, 7–10

Health care acumen, for trainers, 19

Health care data, as needs assessment data source, 24

Health care delivery trends, 3

Health Care Education Association, 132

Health care reform trends, 2

Health maintenance organizations (HMOs): cost and service reduction and, 4; enrollment levels in, 4; regulatory requirements and, 5

Hospitals: accreditation of, 5; consolidation of, 2–3, 7; new delivery models in, 3; reimbursement rate decline for, 4; total quality management (TQM) in, 15; training department structures of, 11–17; training professional roles and responsibilities in, 11–12, 17–18; training services trends in, 9–10

Hospitals and Health Networks, 132

HRD Press, 134

HRDQ (Human Resource Development Quarterly), 133

Human resource systems, competencies and, 37–39

I

Immigration, 6, 8

Individualized development plan (IDP), 39, 40, 56

InFocus machines, 78

Information systems, 3, 4

Integrated structure, 14–15

Intellectual capital, 7

Interactivity, 83

Internal consulting. *See* Consulting

International Society of Performance Improvement, 132

Internet: diagnosis with, 8; patient monitoring on, 4

Interpersonal skills, for trainers, 19. *See also* Facilitation

Interventions: in consulting project, 119, 125, 127; organizational development, examples of, 127

Interviewing skills tests, 94

Interviews: conducting, 25–26, 122–123; guidelines for, 123; for internal consulting project assessment, 122–123; for needs assessment, 24, 25–26, 30, 33–34; for organizational business assessment, 116, 117; pros and cons of, 30; for training transfer evaluation, 95

Introduction to training, 83

Issue statements, 118

J

Jeopardy-style games, 60, 80

Job aids, 65–66, 107

Job analysis, 41

Job descriptions, 25

Joint Commission on Accreditation of Hospitals (JCAHO): charge and task of, 15–16; history of, 16

Joint Commission on Accreditation of Hospitals (JCAHO) requirements, 5; for competencies and competency assessment, 41, 43, 44; course titles based on, 17; education/training-related,

listed, 16; impact of, on training department structures, 11, 15–17; for performance improvement, 6

Jossey-Bass/Pfeiffer, 75, 134

Journals, for continuous learning, 115, 133–134

K

Kirkpatrick, D., 90

L

Language, for training materials, 67

Learning: continuous, for training professionals, 19, 113, 114, 115–116, 129; individualized plan for, 39, 40, 56; trend toward, 7, 10

Learning contract, 98, 100

Learning evaluations, 93–94; example of, 94; guidelines for developing, 93. *See also* Tests

Learning log, 98, 100

Learning methodologies, 58–64; adult learners' needs and, 58–59; engaging, 59–64

Learning needs of health care trainers, 12, 19–20. *See also* Continuous learning

Learning objectives: components of, listed, 55; condition component of, 56; criteria component of, 56; determination of, 55–56; examples of, 56; performance component of, 55–56

Learning organizations, 7, 10; sample training strategic plan for, 116, 117, 118

Learning strategic plan, 116–118

Learning styles, 74–75; defined, 74; visual, 74–75

Learning teams, 10, 64

Lecture method, 61

Lesson plan, 57–58; components of, 58; sample, for blood-drawing, 57–58; sample, for conflict management, 58,

Skill tests, 94
Skills practice, 60
Smile sheets, 90–92
Smiling, 74, 85
Soft skills training, 14, 15
Speaking, 61, 73
Spelling and grammar, 69
Staffing mixes and ratios, 3
Staffing planning competency, 41
Statement of purpose, 54–55
Statement of understanding, 120–122; sample, 120–121
Strategic plans: as needs assessment data source, 24, 25, 30; for training, 116–118
Succession planning, competencies and, 39
Support functions, 3
Surveys or questionnaires: guidelines for creating, 27; for needs assessment, 27–28, 30, 32, 45–48; pros and cons of, 30; sample, for clinical training needs assessment, 32, 49–51; sample, for management development needs assessment, 32, 45–48; sample, for nursing administrators educational needs assessment, 28; for training transfer evaluation, 95, 96
Systemwide education, 12

T
Tactile learning and delivery, 75
Team effectiveness consulting project, 124, 126, 127, 128
Team effectiveness training, 84–85, 102
Teams, learning, 10, 64
Technology skills, need for, 6, 8
Technology trends, 3–4
Television clips, 79
Tests: of competency, 43, 94; developing and administering, 93–94; for learning evaluation, 93–94; as learning methodology, 62; for needs assessment, 29; paper-and-pencil, 93; resources for

construction of, 62, **ch.9; sample questions for, 93. *See also* Competency assessment; Evaluation
Thematic analysis, 30–31
Themes, 81
Time constraints, 101, 102, 105–106
Time guidelines for delivery, 84
Time management problem analysis, 109–110
Toastmasters, 74
Total quality management (TQM), 15
Trainee role in follow-up and transfer of training, 97
Trainers. *See* Training professionals
Training: versus facilitation, 84–85; versus performance, 111
Training aids, 75–81; pointers for, 76; purpose of, 75–76; types of, 76–81
Training and Development, 131
Training appropriateness determination, 107–112. *See also* Needs assessment
Training delivery, 71–87; classroom behavior problems and, 81–82; components of, listed, 72; for different learning styles, 74–75; do's and don'ts for, 82–84; example of, in listening skills training program, 71–72; freshness of, 84; preparation for and rehearsal of, 72, 74, 83–84; presentation skills and techniques for, 71, 73–74; time guidelines for, 84; variety in, 84; visual aids for, 75–81
Training department structures, 11–17; basics of, 13–15; current model of, 12–13; historical evolution of, 15; impact of JCAHO requirements on, 11, 15–17; integrated, 14–15; organizational effectiveness model of, 12–13; parallel, 13–14
Training design, 53–69; content component of, 57–58, 59; evaluation component of, 69, 99; example of, for communication skills program, 53–54; learning

Visual learning and delivery, 74–75
Voice, 71, 73

W
Wheel of Fortune, 60
White space, 67, 76
Wizard of Oz, The, 79, 81

Women in workforce, 6
Work samples, as needs assessment data
    source, 29
Workforce diversity, 6, 8
Workplace trends, 5–7; implications of,
    for health care, 7–10
Workshop planner, sample, 63